民航

民航乘务员客舱广播实用教程

（第二版）

张 菁 高 锋 王 杭 主 编
吴江华 朱 宁 副主编

清华大学出版社
北 京

内 容 简 介

本书根据民航客舱广播情景，辅以案例，详细阐述了普通话、英语发音的基础知识，以及广播基础知识，介绍了民航客舱特情广播、应急广播、基础广播的方法与技巧。与其他教材相比，本书增加了普通话和英语发音的播音技巧、机上广播注意事项以及相关学科的知识等，注重广播词与机上急救医疗、应急处置内容相结合。

本书可作为本科院校和高职院校航空专业、航空公司人员培训的教材，也可供相关专业人员参考。

本书封面贴有清华大学出版社防伪标签，无标签者不得销售。
版权所有，侵权必究。举报：010-62782989，beiqinquan@tup.tsinghua.edu.cn。

图书在版编目（CIP）数据

民航乘务员客舱广播实用教程 / 张菁，高锋，王杭
主编 . -- 2 版 . -- 北京：清华大学出版社，2024.7 (2025.8 重印).
（民航专业融媒体系列教材）. -- ISBN 978-7-302-66838-1

Ⅰ . F560.9
中国国家版本馆 CIP 数据核字第 2024HQ3115 号

责任编辑：杜　晓
封面设计：曹　来
责任校对：李　梅
责任印制：宋　林

出版发行：清华大学出版社
网　　址：https://www.tup.com.cn，https://www.wqxuetang.com
地　　址：北京清华大学学研大厦A座　　　　邮　　编：100084
社 总 机：010-83470000　　　　　　　　　　邮　　购：010-62786544
投稿与读者服务：010-62776969，c-service@tup.tsinghua.edu.cn
质量反馈：010-62772015，zhiliang@tup.tsinghua.edu.cn
课件下载：https://www.tup.com.cn，010-83470410

印 装 者：三河市铭诚印务有限公司
经　　销：全国新华书店
开　　本：185mm×260mm　　印　张：11.5　　字　数：226千字
版　　次：2021年6月第1版　2024年8月第2版　印　次：2025年8月第2次印刷
定　　价：49.00元

产品编号：106963-01

第二版前言

近年来，国家高度重视民航业的发展，将民航业作为推动我国社会经济发展的重要战略产业，这标志着我国民航业进入了以人才为核心的崭新阶段。新阶段的新任务需要我们改变观念、创新教育模式，在此过程中教材的建设更新、与时俱进是首要任务。

近年来，民航业的高速发展对人才培养提出了新的挑战。为了培养服务于民航业发展的高质量人才，国内一些大专高职院校空乘类专业相继开设了"民航客舱广播"这类课程，但是能够比较全面地反映模拟真实航班上的乘务员客舱广播，比较系统地收集具有代表性、权威性的广播词，以高职空乘专业学生双语学习为起点同时又结合了机上广播知识和播音技巧的教材少之又少。以往的教材过于拘泥于广播的形式，很少考虑机上播音技巧、普通话的继续教育、案例、机上广播情景等。本书在此类教材基础上组织教材内容，更贴近实际工作场景，为提高空乘学生的综合素质，提升今后的工作岗位素养，为兄弟院校的创新和个性化教学提供了素材。

本书以突出职业能力语言应用能力培养为目标，这一目标的达成有赖于对企业真实需求的把握和对适用人才能力需求的切实了解。需求分析为职场环境下的普通话、英语语言技能与职业技能培养建立了对接通道。

本书第一版获得"2023年度上海市高职院校经济类专业优秀教材评选"三等奖。本书在改版时主要体现以下特色。

（1）体现双语文化底蕴对机上广播和航空服务语言表达的重要性。通过理论与技巧实践相结合的原则强化空乘专业学生学习广播播音和双语的学习兴趣与观念，提升岗前综合素质。

（2）以模拟机上广播词、全面提升双语素养能力为目标，优化课程内容，满足双语文化底蕴，提升机上实用语言技巧，为空乘专业医疗急救、机上应急处置、航线地理等课程打下基础。

（3）注重三线教学、一课一空间等个性化教学的宗旨，注重双语知识和广播词以及英语教学的融会贯通，让空乘专业的学生在入职前就能模拟机上广播，了解相关案例。

（4）根据高职空乘专业学生的英语学习程度与需求，本专业资深的专业乘务员和英语教师经过认真的讨论研究，将实践经验和专业成果融入书中，引进素质教育理念，打造教材特色。

（5）机上服务理念和专业能力培养并重，旨在培养高层次、高素质的民航服务型人才。

（6）遵循新型教学与专业课程打造理念，结合民航国际化特点，力求创新、务实、与时俱进。本书配有相关音频、教学课件等数字教学资源。

本书在编写时，考虑高职学生的整体学习水平，标记"*"的内容可以作为选学内容，而且由于各高职院校和培训机构的不同，项目一和项目二的学习内容可以视课程情况选学或自学。另外，项目三每节内容建议用 2 课时（每课时 45 分钟），项目四和项目五除带"*"的疫情广播教学为 2 课时外，其余课程均建议用 1 课时。

本书编者为上海旅游高等专科学校张菁、上海民航职业技术学院高锋、中国民航飞行学院空乘学院王杭、上海民航职业技术学院吴江华和上海旅游高等专科学校朱宁。本书由张菁、高锋负责内容结构设计，张菁、王杭负责编写，吴江华、朱宁参与资料收集与整合。

本书在编写过程中，参考了大量文献，在此一并表示感谢。由于编者水平有限，书中不足之处在所难免，请各位读者和教师指正。

编　者

2024 年 3 月

本书配套线上课程

目 录

理 论 篇

项目一　机上广播词播音理论基础 …… 3
　任务一　普通话发音播音技巧 …… 3
　　一、语音基础知识 …… 3
　　二、语言表达 …… 5
　任务二　英语发音与播音技巧 …… 9
　　一、语音基础知识 …… 9
　　二、英语语言表达的规则与技巧 …… 17
　任务三　中英文数字的互译及度量单位 …… 24
　　一、中英文数字互译 …… 25
　　二、中英文时间、度量单位等的转换 …… 27
　任务四　民航乘务员客舱广播技巧及注意事项 …… 31
　　一、客舱广播基本原则 …… 31
　　二、客舱广播技巧 …… 32
　　三、客舱广播注意事项 …… 34

项目二　民航机场与航班广播常识 …… 37
　任务一　机场三字代码 …… 37
　　一、国内部分机场名称及三字代码 …… 38
　　二、国内机场三字代码速记法 …… 39
　　三、部分国际城市三字代码 …… 41
　　四、部分航空公司二字代码 …… 42
　任务二　航线地标 …… 46
　　一、国内部分机场信息 …… 46

二、国外部分机场信息 ········· 47
　　三、国内部分航线地标 ········· 48
　　四、国际部分航线地标 ········· 49
任务三　华氏与摄氏温度换算表及换算法 ········· 51
　　一、两种温标的由来 ········· 51
　　二、两种温标的计算方法 ········· 52
　　三、华氏和摄氏温度换算简表 ········· 53
任务四　各国入境海关检疫规定简述 ········· 55
　　一、中国海关出入境规定 ········· 55
　　二、美国海关入境与申报注意事项 ········· 57
　　三、英国入境和海关检查注意事项 ········· 58
　　四、澳大利亚入境海关检疫规定 ········· 59
　　五、法国入境海关检疫规定 ········· 63
　　六、日本海关对入境所携带物品的规定 ········· 63
　　七、韩国入境海关规定 ········· 63

实　践　篇

项目三　基础广播教学 ········· 69
任务一　乘客登机广播 ········· 69
　　一、乘客登机广播词 ········· 70
　　二、乘客登机情景用语 ········· 71
任务二　关门—滑行广播 ········· 76
　　一、关门—滑行广播词 ········· 77
　　二、关门—滑行情景用语 ········· 78
任务三　国际航班空中服务广播（一）——平飞—落地前供餐广播 ········· 82
　　一、平飞—落地前供餐广播词 ········· 83
　　二、送餐服务情景用语 ········· 85
任务四　国际航班空中服务广播（二）——落地与中转广播 ········· 90
　　一、落地与中转广播词 ········· 91
　　二、预报时间和乘客中转情景用语 ········· 93
任务五　国际航班空中服务广播（三）——检疫入境广播 ········· 97
　　一、检疫入境广播词 ········· 98

二、填写入境卡情景用语 …………………………………………… 100

　任务六　国际航班落地滑行广播 ………………………………………… 104

　　一、落地滑行广播 …………………………………………………… 105

　　二、航班抵达情景用语 ……………………………………………… 107

项目四　特情广播教学 ………………………………………………… 112

　任务一　起飞延误广播 …………………………………………………… 112

　　一、起飞延误广播词 ………………………………………………… 113

　　二、起飞延误情景用语 ……………………………………………… 114

　任务二　落地延误广播 …………………………………………………… 118

　　一、落地延误广播词 ………………………………………………… 118

　　二、中转乘客延误情景用语 ………………………………………… 120

　任务三　特殊事件广播 …………………………………………………… 123

　　一、特殊事件广播词 ………………………………………………… 124

　　二、特殊事件情景用语 ……………………………………………… 127

　*任务四　疫情广播 ………………………………………………………… 131

　　一、疫情广播词 ……………………………………………………… 132

　　二、疫情航班情景用语 ……………………………………………… 135

项目五　应急广播教学 ………………………………………………… 140

　任务一　失火广播 ………………………………………………………… 140

　　一、失火广播词 ……………………………………………………… 141

　　二、客舱失火情景用语 ……………………………………………… 142

　任务二　释压广播 ………………………………………………………… 146

　　一、释压广播词 ……………………………………………………… 146

　　二、客舱释压情景用语 ……………………………………………… 148

　任务三　紧急撤离广播 …………………………………………………… 152

　　一、紧急撤离广播词 ………………………………………………… 152

　　二、紧急撤离情景用语 ……………………………………………… 155

　任务四　安全设备示范广播 ……………………………………………… 160

　　一、安全设备示范广播词 …………………………………………… 160

　　二、安全设备示范情景用语 ………………………………………… 164

附录 ·· 168
    附录一   机上餐食、酒类中英文名称对照表 ························· 168
    ＊附录二   机上急救医疗中英文对照表 ································· 170
    ＊附录三   机上应急处置中英文对照表 ································· 171
    附录四   各国城市中英文简表 ··· 173

参考文献 ·· 174

理 论 篇

项目一
机上广播词播音理论基础

项目目标

知识目标	掌握普通话发音播音技巧； 掌握英语发音与播音技巧； 掌握中英文数字的互评及度量单位； 了解民航乘务员客舱广播技巧及注意事项。
技能目标	熟练运用普通话进行广播； 流利运用英语进行广播； 熟练列举出客舱广播技巧及注意事项。
职业素养目标	培养学生的职业意识和职业素养； 培养专业学生爱岗敬业的精神； 培养学生机上广播的职业技能。

任务一 普通话发音播音技巧

任务导入

普通话是以北京语音为标准音，以北方话为基础方言，以典型的现代白话文为语法规范的通用语。那么如何用标准优美的普通话进行机上中文广播呢？本任务将从提高学生普通话语言能力的角度进行阐述。

任务要求

通过本任务的学习，学习者应基本理解使用普通话广播时应具备的基础知识和简单技巧。

一、语音基础知识

普通话语音系统有声母、韵母、声调等，音节是普通话语音系统的基本单位，一般一个汉字就是一个音节。一个音节由声母、韵母、声调组成；一个音节可以没有声母，但是不能没有韵母和声调。

（一）声母

普通话语音共有 21 个声母，如表 1-1 所示，其中 m、n、l、r 是声带振动的浊音。除表 1-1 所列声母外，还有一种零声母音节，由韵母独立成为音节，如 ā（阿）、ò（哦）、é（额）、ér（儿）、ài（爱）、ào（奥）、ōu（欧）、ān（安）、ēn（恩）、áng（昂）等。

表 1-1　声母表

发音方法		双唇音	唇齿音	舌尖中音	舌尖前音	舌尖后音	舌面前音	舌面后音
塞（sè）音	不送气	b		d				g
	送气	p		t				k
塞擦音	不送气				z	zh	j	
	送气				c	ch	q	
擦音	清音		f		s	sh	x	h
	浊音					r		
鼻音	浊音	m		n				ng
边音	浊音			l				

（1）塞（sè）音——发音部位的某两个部分阻挡气流后，突然打开使气流迸发而出。

（2）塞擦音——发音部位的某两个部分阻挡气流后逐步松开，形成一条缝隙，气流从中挤出。

（3）擦音——发音部位的某两个部分靠近形成一条缝隙，气流从中挤出。

（4）鼻音——发音时软腭下垂，口腔中形成阻挡的两个部位完全闭合，使气流从鼻腔中流出。鼻音都是声带振动的浊音。

（5）边音——舌尖与上齿龈的某一点接触，阻挡气流后，舌头两边放松留有空隙，气流振动声带后从空隙中流出。

（二）韵母

普通话语音共有 39 个韵母，主要由元音充当，也有元音后面带有鼻辅音的。韵母分成单韵母、复韵母、鼻韵母三类。

（1）单韵母由一个元音构成，共 10 个，如表 1-2 所示。

表 1-2　单韵母发音表

舌位高低	舌面母音					舌尖母音		卷舌母音
	前		中	后		前	后	中
	不圆	圆		不圆	圆			
高	i	ü			u	-i [ɿ] [兹]	-i [ʅ] [知]	er
半高				e	o			
中			(e)					
半低	ê							
低	(a)			a	(ɑ)			

（2）复韵母由两个或三个元音组成，共13个：ai、ei、ao、ou、ia、ie、ua、uo、üe、iao、iou、uai、uei。

（3）鼻韵母由元音和鼻辅音构成，元音在前，辅音在后，共16个：an、ian、uan、üan、en、in、uen、ün、ang、iang、uang、eng、ing、ueng、ong、iong。

（三）声调

普通话的每一个音节都有声调，对于声母、韵母相同的音节，会因声调不同，意义就不同。

（1）阴平/第一声：高平调。发音时声音高而平，如：jī（机）、shīgē（诗歌）、xīfāng（西方）。

（2）阳平/第二声：中声调。发音时由中度起音向上扬起，如：jí（及）、shícháng（时常）、xítí（习题）。

（3）上声/第三声：降升调。发音时起音比第一声起音略低，先降后升，形成一个曲折的调型，如：jǐ（挤）、shǐzhě（使者）、xǐlǐ（洗礼）。

（4）去声/第四声：全降调。发音时起音高，随后一直降到最低，如：jì（寄）、shìlì（视力）、xìjù（戏剧）。

二、语言表达

普通话语言表达技巧体现在停连、重音、语气、节奏四个方面。掌握这些技巧能够有助于准确表达广播词中传递的亲切、温馨、紧急、紧张等情感。

（一）停连

停连包括停和连两部分。"停"指停顿，是指思想感情状态的中断乃至延伸；"连"是指连接标点符号不能连接的内容。两者在语言表达中有显示语意、抒发感情的作用，来自语言感情发展变化的要求。停顿用"/",连接用"⌒"表示。

1. 停连的分类

停连可以分为以下 4 类。

（1）区分性停连：词或短语之间、句与句、层与层、部分与部分之间都有区分性停连，如：

下雨天留客天 / 天留我不留。

下雨天留客天 / 天留我不 / 留！

（2）呼应性停连：播读中运用呼应性停连，必须解决哪个词是"呼"，哪个词是"应"，二者如何呼应，如：

现在 / 飞机正在下降。请您回原座位坐好，⌒系好安全带，⌒收起小桌板，⌒调直座椅靠背，⌒拉开遮光板。

（3）并列性停连：语段中处于同等位置、同等关系、同等样式词语之间的连接或者有标点符号，但联系紧密的词语、段落，如：

乐山大佛 / 神秘、⌒雄伟、⌒壮观。

（4）分合性停连：在语句并列关系之前，通常有领属性词语；也会在并列关系之后，有总结性词语。分合性停连比并列性停连时间要长，包括先合后分和先分后合两种情况。如：

为保证/飞行安全,飞行全程中/请您不要使用/手机、⌒笔记本电脑/和其他电子设备。

2. 停连的方式

停连的方式有停顿方式和连接方式。

1）停顿方式

（1）落停，一般用于已完成的句子中，表示一个完整的意思，停顿时间相对较长，句尾声音顺势而落，/ 就表示落停，如：

感谢 / 您的配合。

（2）扬停，一般用于未完成的句子中，一个意思还没有说完，也没有标点符号，但是需要停顿的地方，"/"表示扬停，停顿时间较短，停顿时声音停下气却未尽。扬停之前声音稍微上扬或者拉平，停顿之后的声音缓起或者突起。如：

现在 / 由客舱乘务员为您进行 / 安全设备示范，请您 / 注意观看。

2）连接方式

（1）直连，通常不换气，只用胸中一口余气，用于并列字词紧密的地方，顺势连带，不露接点，如：

旅途中 / 我们将经过 / 湖南、⌒湖北、⌒河南。

（2）曲连，用于较舒缓的内容，用于一句话或者一段话中间的连接，声断意连，环环向前，如：

　　大连 / 是我国著名的沿海游览、⌒疗养胜地，位于辽东半岛，⌒与山东半岛隔海相望，⌒是我国 / 重要的工业城市之一。

（二）重音

重音是语句中表示目的性的字或词语，是最能表达思想感情，体现语句目的。重音不等于重读，要有主次之分，不同的语境重音位置是不同的。广播词的导向是我们选择重音的一个要素，重音用"＿"表示。广播词重音的表达方法有延长字音、提高声音、加大音量 3 种。如：

　　谁喜欢打羽毛球？我喜欢打羽毛球。

　　你喜欢打羽毛球吗？我喜欢打羽毛球。

（三）语气

生活中的每一句话都是有语气的。不同的人表现同一句话的语气内涵和外在都不会完全相同。语气有陈述语气、祈使语气、感叹语气等；说话的腔调、句子中的声音高低变化、快慢轻重都是语调。客舱广播员广播的情感就是语气的灵魂，声音就是语气的载体。

广播的感情色彩对于语气声音的表现形式如下。

（1）热情：气徐声柔、口腔宽松、气息深长。

（2）喜悦：气满声高、口腔似千里行舟、气息不绝清流。

（3）紧张：气短声促、口腔似弓箭、气息穿梭。

（四）节奏

节奏是规律性变化的，不是单一的，有段落才有起伏，有起伏才见节奏。节奏是广播员播音时的情感起伏所造成的抑扬顿挫、轻重缓急的回环往复，是以情感变化为基础的声音的外在表现，具有整体性。

1. 广播的节奏类型

广播的节奏类型包括以下 3 种。

（1）轻快型：多扬少抑、声音不着力，语流中顿挫少、顿挫时间短暂，语速相对较快。

（2）舒缓型：声音轻松明朗、略高不着力，语速徐缓、语势轻柔舒展，适用于大多数的客舱广播。

（3）紧张型：声音多扬少抑、多重少轻，语速快、气息促，顿挫短暂，语言密度大，适用于应急广播和部分特情广播。

2. 节奏的转换方法

节奏的转换方法由声音的高低、轻重、缓急、停连组合成以下 4 种。

（1）欲扬先抑、欲抑先扬。

（2）欲快先慢、欲慢先快。

（3）欲重先轻、欲轻先重。

（4）欲连先停、欲停先连。

3. 节奏转换的技巧

节奏转换的技巧包括以下 6 种。

（1）突转：节奏形式的转换速度快，在内容发生较大、较明显的变化时采用。

（2）大转：与突转相似，一般用于前后内容衔接不是很紧凑的语句、语段。

（3）逆转：内容色彩向相反方向转换，节奏变化的幅度、速度视情况而定。

（4）渐转：缓转慢回，往往节奏比较统一并稍有变化。

（5）小转：节奏虽有转换，但幅度不大，主要是节奏尺度上的变化。

（6）顺转：感情色彩基本一致，节奏、感情从顺向关系的不同角度、不断积累、逐步深化。

知识拓展：普通话的历史沿革

清朝末年已出现"普通话"一词，1909 年清政府规定北京官话为"国语"。国语的前身是明清官话，更早之前则称为"雅言"。

近代，我国多次制定国语读音。1918 年北洋政府公布了第一套国家认可的国语注音字母。1923 年国语统一筹备会第五次会议决定基于近代中国北方官话的白话文语法和北京话语音制定语音。1932 年，国民政府教育部颁布《国音常用字汇》后，确定国语标准。

1953 年我国将北京市、河北省承德市滦（luán）平县作为普通话标准音的主要采集地，制定标准后于 1955 年向全国推广，并规定国家通用语言为普通话。2000 年，《中华人民共和国国家通用语言文字法》确立了普通话和规范汉字作为国家通用语言文字的法律地位。

◆ 任 务 实 践 ◆

（1）简述普通话语音的基础知识。

（2）简述停连的分类和方式。

（3）根据本任务所学内容方法，熟练朗读下段中文广播词，正确标示出停连、重音的符号，使用正确的节奏和语气。

➡ 回收耳机广播词 ⬅

女士们、先生们：

飞机马上就要到达____机场，我们的音乐娱乐节目即将结束，请将耳机交还给客舱乘务员，谢谢！

（注：国际中远程等航线，经济舱的耳机是平飞后发放给乘客的，在落地广播前，为了安全，耳机等松散物品由乘务员收回。）

任务二　英语发音与播音技巧

任务导入

在长期的传播过程中，英语形成了具有地方特色的发音特点。但是，在国际音标的范畴下，英语发音仍有一套较为完整的体系，掌握这些知识与规则，并在实践中注重跟读和模仿，体会、训练、掌握并运用发音与播音的技巧，能够有效提升学生的英语语音和语调的准确性。

任务要求

通过对本任务的学习，学习者应了解英语语音的基础知识、基本规则和技巧，并能运用到英语播音的训练和工作中。

一、语音基础知识

英语语音的基础知识包括音素、音标、音节[①]。

音素（phoneme）是根据语音的自然属性划分出来的最小语音单位，依据发音动作来分析，一个动作构成一个音素。音素分为元音音素与辅音音素两大类。

由于音素是语音（声音）单位，可听但不可视。因此，为了便于记录，我们用文字符号将音素表示出来，并放在双斜线"//"中间，称为音标，如 /e/，双斜线中间的"e"即

[①] 在语言学研究领域，英语语音与英语话语的基础知识和基本规则涉及更广泛、更精深的内容，在本书中，我们仅就最基本的常用内容进行学习。有兴趣的教师和同学可自主学习相关内容。

是元音音素"e"的文字书写。

音节是比音素更大的语音单位,是读音的基本单位,任何单词的读音都可以分解为一个个的音节朗读。一个元音音素可构成一个音节,一个元音音素和一个或几个辅音音素结合也可以构成一个音节,辅音音素通常不能单独构成音节,但 /m/、/n/、/l/ 这 3 个辅音是响音,它们和辅音音素结合,也可构成音节。

(一)音素

英语中有 26 个字母,但是却有 48 个音素(或 44 个,国内普遍采用 48 个)。其中元音音素 20 个,辅音音素 28 个(或 24 个)。元音,发音清晰响亮,发音过程中,气流不会受到任何阻碍;辅音,发音相对模糊微弱。发音过程中,气流在通过咽喉、口腔的过程中,会在不同程度上受到不同部位的阻碍,气流必须克服各种阻碍,才能成音。

1. DJ 音标

英国语音学家 Daniel Jones(1881—1967)根据国际音标(International Phonetic Alphabet,IPA)编写了一本英国英语的发音辞典《英语正音辞典》(English Pronouncing Dictionary)。通常我们所说的英语音标,即英式发音的国际音标,就是用他姓名的首字母缩写 DJ 来表示的,即 DJ 音标。国内普遍采用 DJ 音标的修订版作为英语国际音标的标准版本,即包含 48 个音素,其中 20 个元音音素,28 个辅音音素[①]。我们将通过两种方式对这些音素进行分类展示,为严谨起见,我们仍将这些音素置于双斜线中间,形式上是音标,内容上强调音素。

(1)第一种分类方法便于记忆,按照发音特点进行分类,如表 1-3 和表 1-4 所示。

表 1-3 元音音素[②](20 个)

长元音	/ɑ:/	/ɔ:/	/ɜ:/	/i:/	/u:/		
短元音	/ʌ/	/ɒ/	/ə/	/ɪ/	/ʊ/	/e/	/æ/
双元音	/eɪ/	/aɪ/	/ɔɪ/				
	/ɪə/	/eə/	/ʊə/				
	/əʊ/	/aʊ/					

表 1-4 辅音音素(28 个)

轻辅音	/p/	/t/	/k/	/f/	/s/	/θ/	/ʃ/	/tʃ/	/ts/	/tr/
浊辅音	/b/	/d/	/g/	/v/	/z/	/ð/	/ʒ/	/dʒ/	/dz/	/dr/
鼻音	/m/	/n/	/ŋ/							

① 近代的语言学家认为 DJ 音标中的 /tr/ /dr/ /ts/ /dz/ 是一种辅音连缀,而并非不同的音位,因此将传统 DJ 音标表中的清辅音(/tr/ /ts/)和对应的浊辅音(/dr/ /dz/)删除,实现了与美式音标的辅音完全一致,均为 24 个辅音。但国内普遍采用修订版的 DJ 音标,即 48 个音素。

② 国际音标的书写,在不同阶段产生了不同的变化,本书按照传统的书写方式来标注,但在不同的教材或资料中,会出现同一音素的不同写法。主要包括 /ɪ/ 与 /i/、/ɜ:/ 与 /ə:/、/ʊ/ 与 /u/、/ɒ/ 与 /ɔ/ 等。

续表

半元音	/j/	/w/				
舌侧音	/l/					
其他	/h/	/r/				

（2）第二种分类方法便于发音练习，元音音素按照发音部位分类如表 1-5 所示，辅音音素按照发音方式分类，如表 1-6 所示。

表 1-5　元音音素（20 个）

单元音	前元音	/iː/	/ɪ/	/æ/	/e/	
	中元音	/ɜː/	/ə/			
	后元音	/ɑː/	/ʌ/	/uː/	/ʊ/	/ɔː/	/ɒ/
双元音	合口双元音	/aɪ/	/eɪ/	/ɔɪ/	/aʊ/	/əʊ/
	集中双元音	/ɪə/	/eə/	/ʊə/		

表 1-6　辅音音素（28 个）

爆破音	/p/	/t/	/k/	/b/	/d/	/g/
摩擦音	/f/	/v/	/θ/	/ð/	/ʃ/	/ʒ/
	/s/	/z/	/h/	/r/		
破擦音	/ts/	/tʃ/	/tr/	/dz/	/dʒ/	/dr/
鼻辅音	/m/	/n/	/ŋ/			
半元音	/j/	/w/				
舌侧音	/l/					

2. 发音方法

发音部位参照图 1-1 和图 1-2。

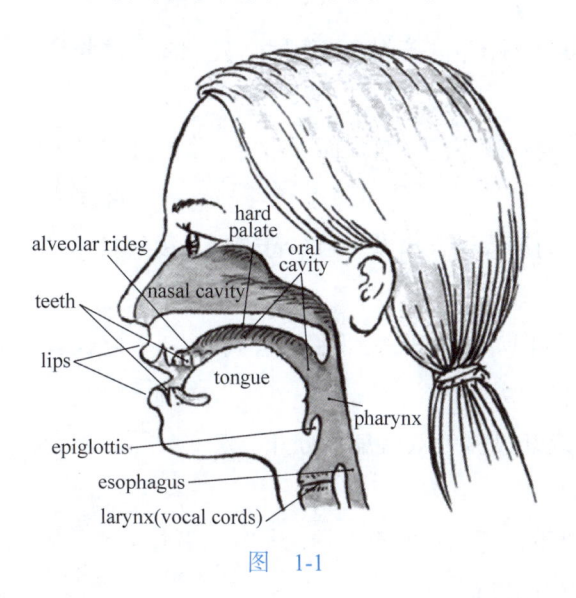

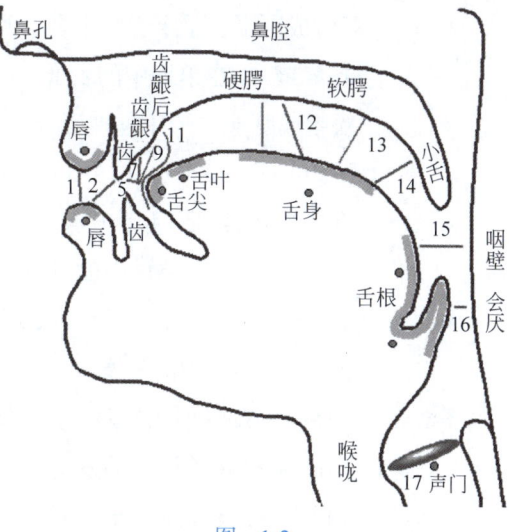

图　1-1

图　1-2

（1）元音

- /iː/：舌抵下齿，双唇扁平做微笑状，发"一"之长音，是字母 ea、ee、ey、ie，或 ei 在单词中的发音，此音是长元音，一定注意把音发足。
- /ɪ/：舌抵下齿，双唇扁平分开，牙床近于全舌，发短促之"一"音，是字母 i 或 y 在单词中的发音，发此音要短促而轻快。
- /æ/：双唇扁平，舌前微升，舌尖抵住下龈，牙床开，软腭升起，唇自然开放，是字母 a 在闭音节或重读闭音节中的发音。
- /e/：舌近硬腭，舌尖顶下齿，牙床半开半合，做微笑状，是字母 e 或 ea 在单词中的发音。
- /ɜː/：舌上抬，唇成自然状态，口半开半闭，发"厄"之长音，是字母 er、ir、or 或 ur 在单词中的发音。
- /ə/：舌上抬，唇成自然状态，口半开半闭，发"厄"之短音，是字母 a、o、u、e、or、er 或 ur 在单词中的发音。
- /ɑː/：双唇张而不圆，牙床大开，舌后微升，舌尖向后升缩微离下齿，发"阿"之长音。是字母 er 在闭音节或重读闭音节中的发音，也是字母 a 在以 st 结尾的单词中的发音。
- /ʌ/：双唇平放，牙床半开，舌尖抵住下龈，舌后微微升起，发短促之"阿"音，是字母 o 或 u 在单词中的发音。
- /ɔː/：双唇界于开闭、圆唇之间，牙床半开渐至全开，舌尖卷上再过渡为卷后，是字母 o、al、or、oar、our 或 oor 在单词中的发音。
- /ɒ/：双唇稍微向外突出圆形，舌后升起，舌尖不触下齿，发"噢"短音，是字母 o 在单词中的发音。
- /uː/：双唇成圆形，牙床近于半合，舌尖不触下齿，自然而不用力，发"屋"之长音，是字母 oo 或 ou 在单词中的发音。
- /ʊ/：双唇成圆形，牙床近于半合，舌尖不触下齿，自然而不用力，发短促之"屋"音，是字母 u、oo 或 ou 在单词中的发音。
- /aɪ/：将口张开略圆，舌后升起，舌尖向后收缩，由发"阿"音平稳过渡到发"一"音，是字母 i 或 y 在单词中的发音。
- /eɪ/：舌尖顶下齿，牙床半开半合，双唇扁平，由发"哀"平稳过渡到发"一"之长音，是字母 a 在开音节中的发音。
- /ɔɪ/：双唇外突成圆形，发"噢"音逐渐过渡为双唇扁平分开，发"一"之短音，是字母 oy 和 oi 在单词中的发音。
- /ɪə/：双唇张开，牙床由窄至半开，舌抵下齿逐渐过渡至上卷，从"一"音过渡到"厄"音，是字母 ear、ere、ea、eer 在单词中的发音。

- /eə/：双唇张开后略圆，牙床张开相当宽，舌尖卷上渐至卷后，是字母 ear、are、air 在单词中的发音。
- /ʊə/：双唇成圆形，牙床近于半合，舌尖不触下齿，发"屋"之长音，然后从"屋"音过渡到"厄"音，是字母 our、oor、ure、eer 在单词中的发音。
- /aʊ/：将口张开略圆，渐渐合拢，双唇成圆形，由发"阿"音平稳过渡到发"屋"音，是字母 ou 和 ow 在单词中的发音。
- /əʊ/：口半开半合，舌后微升，过渡成双唇成圆形，发"欧"之长音，是字母 o、oa 和 oe 在单词中的发音。

（2）辅音

- /p/：双唇紧闭并使气流突破双唇冲出口腔，发音时声带不振动。
- /b/：双唇紧闭并使气流突破双唇冲出口腔，发音时声带振动。
- /t/：双唇微开，先用舌尖抵上齿龈，然后突然张开，使气流冲出口腔发音，发音时声带不振动。
- /d/：双唇微开，先用舌尖抵上齿龈，然后突然张开，使气流冲出口腔发音，发音时声带振动。
- /k/：舌后部隆起，紧贴软腭，形成阻碍，然后突然离开，使气流冲出口腔发音，发音时声带不振动。
- /g/：舌后部隆起，紧贴软腭，形成阻碍，然后突然离开，使气流冲出口腔发音，发音时声带振动。
- /f/：上齿轻触下唇，用力将气流由唇齿之缝隙间吹出，发音时声带不振动。
- /v/：上齿轻触下唇，用力将气流由唇齿之缝隙间吹出，发音时声带振动。
- /s/：双唇微开，上下齿接近于合拢状态，舌尖抵住下齿龈，将气流从牙缝送出，发音时声带不振动。
- /z/：双唇微开，上下齿接近于合拢状态，舌尖抵住下齿龈，将气流从牙缝送出，发音时，声带振动。
- /θ/：上下齿咬舌尖，送出气流，并使舌齿互相摩擦，发音时声带不振动。
- /ð/：上下齿咬舌尖，送出气流，并使舌齿互相摩擦，发音时声带振动。
- /ʃ/：双唇微开，向前突出，舌尖升近上齿龈，用力将气息送出来，发音时声带不振动。
- /ʒ/：双唇微开，向前突出，舌尖升近上齿龈，用力将气息送出来，发音时声带振动。
- /tʃ/：双唇微开，先用舌尖抵上齿龈，突然张开，使气流冲出口腔发音，发音时声带不振动。
- /dʒ/：双唇微开，先用舌尖抵上齿龈，突然张开，使气流冲出口腔发音，发音时声带振动。

- /ts/：舌尖抵住上齿，做好发"t"的姿势，气流冲破阻碍，发出短促的"t"音后，紧接着就发"s"之摩擦音。
- /dz/：舌尖抵住上齿，做好发"d"的姿势，气流冲破阻碍，发出短促的"d"音后，紧接着就发"z"之摩擦音。
- /tr/：舌尖抵住上齿，做好发"tʃ"的姿势，气流冲破阻碍，发出短促的"t"音后，紧接着就发"r"之摩擦音。
- /dr/：舌尖抵住上齿，做好发"dʒ"的姿势，气流冲破阻碍，发出短促的"d"音后，紧接着就发"r"之摩擦音。
- /m/：双唇闭拢，舌放平，使气流从鼻腔出来，发音时声带振动。
- /n/：双唇微闭，舌尖抵住上齿龈，使气流从鼻腔出来，发音时声带振动。
- /ŋ/：软腭下垂，堵住口腔通道，使气息由鼻孔流出来，发音时声带振动。
- /j/：双唇微开，舌抵下齿贴近硬腭，气流摩擦而出，并立即转向其后的元音。
- /w/：双唇突出，呈尖圆形，舌后升向软腭，气息流过，发音时声带振动，并立即转向其后的元音。
- /l/：双唇微开，舌抵上齿龈，气流侧出，发音时声带振动。
- /r/：唇形稍圆，舌身略凹，舌尖上卷，发音时声带振动。
- /h/：口半闭，气息由声门出来，但是发音时声带不振动。

（二）音标

音标通俗地讲，类似于汉语的拼音。如汉字"城"的拼音是 chéng，英语单词 plane 的音标是 /pleɪn/。两者的不同之处是，汉语拼音中，汉字和拼音一一对应；而在英语中，26 个字母各有各的音标（见表 1-7），而不同的字母又可以组合成单词，单词又有各自的读音。

表 1-7　26 个英文字母的音标标注

A /eɪ/	B /biː/	C /siː/	D /diː/	E /iː/	F /ef/	G /dʒiː/
H /eɪtʃ/	I /aɪ/	J /dʒeɪ/	K /keɪ/	L /el/	M /em/	N /en/
O /əʊ/	P /piː/	Q /kjuː/	R /ɑː/	S /es/	T /tiː/	
U /juː/	V /viː/	W /ˈdʌblju:/	X /eks/	Y /waɪ/	Z /ziː/ /zed/	

按照相同的元音音素，可以对 26 个字母进行如表 1-8 所示的分类。

有些单词的读音非常简单，甚至和字母的读音相同，只有一个元音音素或一个辅音音素加一个元音音素。例如，英语单词 eye 和字母 I 的音标都是 /aɪ/，单词 are，ah 和字母 R 的音标都是 /ɑː/，单词 you 和字母 U 的音标都是 /juː/。

表 1-8　按元音音素将 26 个字母进行的分类

/eɪ/	A	H	J	K					
/iː/	B	C	D	E	G	P	T	V	Z（/ziː/）
/e/	F	L	M	N	S	X	Z（/zed/）		
/aɪ/	I	Y							
/uː/	Q	U	W						
/əʊ/	O								
/ɑː/	R								

单词 air 的音标为双元音 /eə/；单词 ear 的音标为双元音 /ɪə/；单词 no 的音标是辅音 /n/ 与元音 /əʊ/ 的组合，即 /nəʊ/；now 的音标是 /n/ 与元音 /aʊ/ 的组合，即 /naʊ/；hi 和 high 是辅音 /h/ 与元音 /aɪ/ 的组合，即 /haɪ/。英语中的所有单词的音标均为上述 48 个音素的拼读组合，有些单词的读音可能需要若干个辅音＋元音的组合，也就构成了多音节词。

（三）音节

音节（syllable）是单个元音音素发音、单个元音音素与单个或多个辅音音素组合发音所构成的最小语音单位，判断音节的关键要点即在于判断元音音素。我们通常认为，一个发音组合中含有一个元音音素，即一个音节；一个发音组合中必须含有一个元音音素，才能构成一个音节。也就是辅音音素或辅音音素＋辅音音素，不能构成音节，但辅音 /m/、/n/、/l/ 是响音，它们和辅音音素结合，也可构成音节，常见的如 /tʃn/、/ʃn/、/tn/、/vl/、/bl/、/ml/。

只含有一个音节的单词称为单音节词；含有两个音节的单词称为双音节词；含有三个及以上音节的单词称为多音节词。双音节词中的音节需要区分重读音节和非重读音节；多音节词中的音节也需要区分重读音节、非重读音节，有时还包括次重读音节。重读音节的符号为"ˈ"，置于重读音节之前的左上角；次重读音节的符号为"ˌ"，置于次重读音节之前的左下角。划分音节的方法通常可以描述为：从左向右，以一个元音加上其左边的辅音为一个音节；如果该元音前面没有辅音，那它就是一个独立的音节；如果两个元音相连，就视为两个音节。

1. 单音节词

单音节词如表 1-9 所示。

表 1-9　单音节词及音标

/iː/	eat/iːt/	bee/biː/	beat/biːt/
/ɪ/	it/ɪt/	big/bɪg/	pitch/pɪtʃ/
/æ/	am/æm/	bag/bæg/	pack/pæk/
/e/	egg/eg/	bed/bed/	left/left/

续表

/ɑː/	arm/ɑːm/	car/kɑː/	branch/brɑːntʃ/
/ʌ/	up/ʌp/	bus/bʌs/	blunt/blʌnt/
/ɜː/	earth/ɜːθ/	nurse/nɜːs/	skirt/skɜːt/
/ə/	of/əv/	the/ðə/	was/wəz/
/ɔː/	or/ɔː/	warm/wɔːm/	small/smɔːl/
/ɒ/	on/ɒn/	blog/blɒg/	strong/strɒŋ/
/uː/	ooze/uːz/	June/dʒuːn/	group/gruːp/
/ʊ/	to/tʊ/	look/lʊk/	wolf/wʊlf/
/aɪ/	aisle/aɪl/	try/traɪ/	flight/flaɪt/
/eɪ/	age/eɪdʒ/	grape/greɪp/	change/tʃeɪndʒ/
/ɔɪ/	oil/ɔɪl/	boy/bɔɪ/	noise/nɔɪz/
/ɪə/	ear/ɪə/	year/jɪə/	beard/bɪəd/
/eə/	air/eə/	hair/heə/	square/skweə/
/ʊə/	tour/tʊə/	poor/pʊə/	sure/ʃʊə/
/aʊ/	out/aʊt/	brown/braʊn/	ground/graʊnd/
/əʊ/	old/əʊld/	know/nəʊ/	throat/θrəʊt/

2. 双音节词

双音节词如表 1-10 所示，其中有一个音节需要重读，而另一个音节保持弱读（也有次重读音节，如表 1-10 中的 online）。通常情况下，动词性的双音节词，第二个音节重读，其他词性的双音节词第一个音节重读，但也不是绝对的。读者还是应该根据音标中重音符号来决定。

表 1-10 双音节词及其音标

/iː/	eaten/ˈiːtən/	beetle/ˈbiːtl/	beaten/ˈbiːtn/
/ɪ/	inform/ɪnˈfɔːm/	bigot/ˈbɪgət/	pitcher/ˈpɪtʃə/
/æ/	ambient/ˈæmbɪənt/	baggage/ˈbægɪdʒ/	packet/ˈpækɪt/
/e/	eggplant/ˈegplɑːnt/	bedroom/ˈbedruːm/	level/ˈlevl/
/ɑː/	army/ˈɑːmi/	cargo/ˈkɑːgəʊ/	blanket/ˈblæŋkɪt/
/ʌ/	upset/ʌpˈset/	bloody/ˈblʌdi/	bluntly/ˈblʌntli/
/ɜː/	earthly/ˈɜːθli/	nurser/ˈnɜːsə/	skirting/ˈskɜːtɪŋ/
/ə/	worker/ˈwəːkə/	apply/əˈplaɪ/	towards/təˈwɔːdz/
/ɔː/	order/ˈɔːdə/	warmer/ˈwɔːmə/	smallpox/ˈsmɔːlpɒks/
/ɒ/	online/ˌɒnˈlaɪn/	beyond/bɪˈjɒnd/	strongly/ˈstrɒŋli/
/uː/	oozy/ˈuːzi/	classroom/ˈklɑːsruːm/	grouper/ˈgruːpə/
/ʊ/	goodwill/ˌgʊdˈwɪl/	looking/ˈlʊkɪŋ/	wolfram/ˈwʊlfrəm/
/aɪ/	island/ˈaɪlənd/	dryer/ˈdraɪə/	flighty/ˈflaɪti/

续表

/eɪ/	famous/ˈfeɪməs/	danger/ˈdeɪndʒə/	afraid/əˈfreɪd/
/ɔɪ/	oily/ˈɔɪli/	boycott/ˈbɔɪkɒt/	noisy/ˈnɔɪzi/
/ɪə/	nearly/ˈnɪəli/	pearson/ˈpɪəsən/	dearest/ˈdɪərɪst/
/eə/	aircraft/ˈeəkrɑːft/	hairdress/ˈheədres/	squarely/ˈskweəli/
/ʊə/	tourist/ˈtʊərɪst/	purely/ˈpjʊəli/	ensure/ɪnˈʃʊə/
/aʊ/	outside/aʊtˈsaɪd/	brownish/ˈbraʊnɪʃ/	grounded/ˈɡraʊndɪd/
/əʊ/	only/ˈəʊnli/	holey/ˈhəʊli/	throwing/ˈθrəʊɪŋ/

3. 多音节词

多音节词如表 1-11 所示，即由三个及三个以上的音节构成的单词。在读这些单词的时候，可以按照音节的个数将其进行分解、然后拼读，拼读过程中要特别注意重读音节和次重读音节。通常情况下，多音节词的重音一般落在倒数第三个音节上，倒数第五个音节是次重音。应该以单词所给的音标为准进行训练。

表 1-11 多音节词

三音节词	frustration/frʌˈstreɪʃn/ statistics/stəˈtɪstɪks/ library/ˈlaɪbrəri/
四音节词	aluminum/ˌæljəˈmɪniəm/ grammatical/ɡrəˈmætɪkl/ absolutely/ˈæbsəluːtli/
五音节词	egotistical/ˌeɡəˈtɪstɪk(ə)l/ cosmopolitan/ˌkɒzməˈpɒlɪtən/ encyclopedia/ɪnˌsaɪkləˈpiːdiə/ particularly/pəˈtɪkjələli/
六音节词	internationally/ˌɪntəˈnæʃnəli/ unnecessarily/ʌnˈnesəsərəli/ particularity/pəˌtɪkjuˈlærəti/ participational/pɑːˌtɪsɪˈpeɪʃənəl/
七音节词	internationalization/ˌɪntəˌnæʃnəlaɪˈzeɪʃn/ accumulativeness/əˈkjuːmjələtɪvnəs/ enthusiastically/ɪnˌθjuːziˈæstɪkəli/
八音节单词	incomprehensibility/ɪnˌkɒmprɪˌhensəˈbɪləti/

二、英语语言表达的规则与技巧

在准确发音的基础上，对英语口语表达的基本规则和技巧用心学习、模仿、训练、掌握并熟练应用，英语播音才能具备英语味道。英语口头表达的基本规则包括重音、节奏和语调。英语口语表达的技巧主要是指连读，连读又分为辅音＋元音连读、元音＋元音连读、辅音＋辅音连读等。

（1）重音是指根据不同的交际需要对句中的某个词或某些词加以强调，使这些词呈现出发音用力较多、音量较大、时间较长、辨识度较清晰的特点。

（2）节奏是指有规律的突变。英语的话语特征是重音突出，重音和轻音（非重音）以特有的规律形成节奏。把握好英语的话语节奏，不仅有助于听懂和理解对方的话语，也有助于让己方的话语表述得清晰易懂。

（3）语调是指话语中音调的高低变化，主要包括升调、降调，多用于表达说话人的思想感情。

（4）连读是指在谈话尤其是自然的语流中，句子或短语中相邻的词之间的连接。通常表现为句子中（尤其是同一意群中）的重读与非重读单词的连续，词与词之间的过渡自然不间断。

（5）失爆又称"失去爆破"，当一个爆破音跟另一个爆破音相遇时往往失去爆破，这主要是因为两个辅音之间的间隔太小，这种现象在语音学上称为"失去爆破"或"特殊爆破"。

（6）句尾辅音弱读是指位于句子末尾的辅音音素，通常只需要摆正发音口型，音长发到音素的三分之一即可。

（一）重音

一个双音节或多音节单词中有重读音节和非重读音节，同理，一个句子中也有重读单词和非重读单词。我们将部分单词需要重读的现象称为句子的重音，重音对于表达思想感情起着重要的作用。无论是汉语还是英语，句中的关键信息（关键词）通常都要读作重音，英语句子重音的一般规律是：实词重读，虚词不重读，但有时为了强调，句子中的任何词都可以读作重音。基本的规则是，句子的重音总是落在需要重读的单词的重读音节上。

实词通常包括动词、名词、形容词、副词、数词、疑问词和感叹词等，这些词通常传递了句子的主要信息，因此需要重读。虚词，包括冠词、介词、连词、物主代词、关系代词、关系副词和助动词等，这些词的主要功能是连接传递信息的实词，形成符合语法的句子，通常不需要重读。但在特定情景中，任何需要强调的词汇，都需要重读。

请根据重音符号，朗读下列句子。

（1）'John 'wants to 'see the 'teacher after 'class.

（2）It's a 'dull and disap'pointing film.

（3）He 'bought 'ten 'cups and 'I bought only 'four.

（4）I've 'never 'heard of 'such a thing be'fore。

（5）He 'lives in a 'house 'not 'far from the 'school.

（6）It's an 'hour's 'drive from the 'old 'station.

（7）The 'girl who 'spoke to you just 'now is my 'sister.

（8）Neither 'you nor 'I can 'solve the 'problem.

（9）I sug'gest that we 'give 'up the 'plan.

（10）The pro'fessor was 'busy 'writing when I 'went to 'see him.

（二）节奏

语言学家将语言节奏分为音节定时节奏和重音定时节奏：每个音节出现的时间间隔相等，则为音节定时节奏；重读音节出现的时间间隔相等，则为重音定时节奏。汉语大致具有音节定时节奏，但英语则属于典型的"按重音定时"的语言。这就是说，英语的话语节奏是一种有规则的节拍，即重读音节出现的时间间隔基本相等。这就意味着，如果两个重读音节之间的非重读音节越多，则这些非重读音节就要读得越快。

英语话语的重音节奏规律是：重读音节与非重读音节相间出现；重读音节与紧跟其后的非重读音节一起组成重音组，而且话语中重音之间的间隔时间大致相等。也就是说，如果句中重读音节出现的频率较高，则语速通常会慢一些，音节听起来更清楚。如果句中非重读音节的数量较多，则语速通常会快一些，音节听起来较含糊。例如：

（1）'Right or 'wrong?　　He is 'right but she is 'wrong.

（2）A 'good 'boy.　　She is 'good to 'boys.

（3）'Blue 'sky.　　It's 'blue in the 'sky.

上述三组例句，虽然总的音节数差别较大（左侧为2~3个，右侧为5~7个），但句中或短语中的重音均为2个。这就要求，读完每组中的两个句子所耗费的时间应基本一致，这就意味着右侧句子中的非重音词汇需要弱读，且语速较快。

同理，在一个相对较长的句子中，重音之间的非重读词汇（音节）数量虽然不同，却要在基本相同的时间间隔内读完这些非重读音节。例如：

（1）He 'turned 'left at the 'end of the 'road.

（2）Does anybody 'doubt that he would be 'able to 'finish it as 'scheduled.

（3）I should have 'thought that 'he could 'get here in time.

在第一句中，turned left 均为重音，需要放慢语速，清晰响亮，留有一定的时间间隔；而 at the 和 of the 作为非重音词汇，需要加快语速，模糊弱读，使这两个音节的发音时长基本等于 turned 和 left 之间所留的时间间隔。同理，第二句中非重音的"that he would be"应与"does anybody"和"it as"的发音时长基本相等。

（三）语调

语调可以使话语的含义完整、明确。说话的内容和说话的方式加在一起才能使话语完整。同样一句话用不同的语调说出来，所表达的含义也不相同。掌握不同语调背后的话语含义，有助于正确地理解和表达。

1. 升调（↗）

升调表示说话人对话语内容的不确定、不完整，通常需要听话人给予确认；也可以表示说话人的话尚未说完，还要继续。升调所表达思想感情相对委婉，常用于表示请求或劝说的疑问句或祈使句。

（1）A：John, can you bring me the bag-pack?

　　　B：Sorry?（↗）（表示没听清，请求对方再说一遍）

（2）You can get here on time, can't you?（↗）（表示疑问，向对方请求确认）

（3）Mr. Johnson lent money to Jack Brown?（↗）（表示惊讶或疑问）

2. 降调（↘）

降调表示说话人对话语内容的确定性和完整性。通常用于陈述句、特殊疑问句以及表示命令的祈使句和感叹句中。

（1）A：John, can you bring me the bag-pack?

　　　B：Sorry.（↘）（表示拒绝）

（2）I'm sorry to keep you waiting for so long time.（↘）（表示陈述，真诚道歉）

（3）Mr. Johnson lent money to Jack Brown.（↘）（陈述事实）

在现实的交际中，升调和降调可以融合在一起使用。融合使用既可以在相邻的句子间，也可以在同一个句子中，表示对不同内容的情感态度，如对比、警告、保留意见、言外有意等。当重音和升降调结合在一起时，则质疑或确认的对象也就有所不同。

（四）连读

连读就是把位于前一个单词的最后一个音与位于后一个单词的第一个音自然地连接起来进行拼读，使说话人的话语更加流利自然。但通常发生在同一个意群（指一个句子中，根据意思和语法结构可将其分成若干个小的单位，每个单位就是一个意群），同一个意群中的词与词关系紧密，不能随意拆分，句子的"停顿"通常在意群之间，因此，连读不能跨意群。

连读通常包括以下几种情况。为了便于观察，我们用弧线（‿）标出连读的音。

1. 辅音 + 元音

前一个单词以辅音结尾，后一个单词以元音开头时，这两个音可以连读。

（1）Take‿a look‿at‿it.

（2）I'll be back in half‿an‿hour.

（3）Will‿it take‿a lot‿of time to go to town on foot?

2. 元音 + 元音

前一个单词以元音结尾，后一个单词以元音开头时，直接连读，中间不做停顿。有时会形成双元音，或半元音音素 /w/ 和 /r/+ 元音的读音。

（1）Don't worry‿about it.

（2）I have waited for you three‿hours.

（3）We‿all agree with the plan.

3. 辅音 + 辅音

前一个单词的词尾辅音与后一个单词的词首辅音相遇，前一个单词的词尾辅音通常只要摆好口型，无须发音，直接将后一个的词首辅音发出即可。

（1）I hope‿to find a good job.

（2）It's not far‿away from here.

（3）Hearing the bad news I couldn't help‿crying.

（4）I live in a two-bedroom‿flat with my parents.

*（五）爆破音

爆破音和爆破音或其他的辅音相邻，第一个爆破音只保留发音动作，但不发生爆破音，称为不完全爆破。说话时，前一个单词的爆破音只保持发音部位（音不发出来）的同时，即向下一个单词起音的辅音过渡，不完全爆破得以实现。

1. 爆破音 + 爆破音

6 个爆破音，即 /b/ /p/ /d/ /t/ /g/ /k/ 中的任意两个相邻时，第一个爆破音不发出爆破音，只保留发音动作，稍微停顿一下，快速向第二个完全爆破的爆破音滑去；若爆破音在词尾则必须轻化。例如：

（1）kept/blackboard/notebook/goodbye/September/suitcase

（2）big boy/sharp pencil/What time?

（3）She took good care of the children.

（4）Ask Bob to sit behind me.

（5）My father kept working till midnight.

（6）I'd like to say goodbye to everyone.

2. 爆破音 + 摩擦音

爆破音后紧跟着的是摩擦音如 /s/ /z/ /ʃ/ /ʒ/ /θ/ /ð/ /f/ /v/ /h/ 时，这种辅音组合在语音学里称为摩擦爆破。换言之，发爆破音时受后面的摩擦音的影响爆破部位有所改变，须由口腔爆破改为摩擦爆破。爆破音和摩擦音相邻，第一个爆破音形成阻碍，发生不完全爆破。例如：

（1）advance/success

（2）a good view/old friends/just then/get through/make sure/night show/keep silence

（3）You must pay in advance.

（4）What would your advice be in this case?

（5）Keep that in mind.

3. 爆破音 + 破擦音

爆破音后面紧跟着的是破擦音 /t/ /tʃ/ /ts/ /dz/ /tr/ /dr/ 时，这种辅音组合在语音学里称为破擦爆破。换言之，发爆破音时受后面的破擦音的影响爆破部位有所改变，须由口腔爆破改为破擦爆破。爆破音和摩擦音相邻，爆破音形成阻碍，失去爆破，稍停顿一下，立刻发出后面的破擦音。例如：

（1）picture/object/grandchild/that child/good job/great changes

（2）I had my picture taken yesterday.

（3）He stood up and objected in strong language.

4. 舌边爆破音

爆破音 /t/ /d/ 后面紧跟着的时舌侧音 /l/ 时，这种辅音组合在语音学里称为舌边爆破。换言之，发爆破音 /t/ /d/ 时受后面舌侧音 /l/ 的影响爆破部位有所改变，须由口腔爆破改为舌边爆破。爆破音和舌侧音 /l/ 相邻，爆破音形成阻碍，发生不完全爆破，例如：

（1）lately/badly/mostly/friendly

（2）a bit louder/I'd like to/straight line/good luck/at last

（3）I have been very busy lately.

（4）He slept badly.

5. 鼻腔爆破音

爆破音和鼻辅音 /m/ /n/ /ŋ/ 相邻，爆破音形成阻碍，发生不完全爆破，在词末必须通过鼻腔爆破。如：爆破音 /t/ /d/ 后面紧跟着的是鼻辅音 /m/ 与 /n/ 时，这种辅音组合在语音学里就称为鼻腔爆破。换言之，发爆破音 /t/ /d/ 时，受后面鼻辅音 /m/ 与 /n/ 的影响爆破部位有所改变，须由口腔爆破改为鼻腔爆破。例如，button、garden 中的 /t/ /d/ 就得采取上述方法发音，说得通俗一点也就是 /t/ /d/ 的发音由原爆破音改道从鼻子里带出来，也就是由鼻腔爆破发出来，因此在发音时鼻子里（不是口腔）会有一种充气和痒的感觉。

（1）utmost/admit/midnight

（2）good night/good morning/take time/start now/don't know/just moment

（3）He often comes home at midnight.

（4）He has always been a good neighbor.

6．浊化音

辅音在重读时要读成其相对的浊辅音，如 /s/ 后面的清辅音要浊化，即在 /s/ 后面，如果跟的是 /p/ /k/ 和 /t/ 等清辅音，可以相应的被浊化成 /b/ /g/ 和 /d/ 等，注意浊化不能过于浊，不然容易与和浊辅音混淆。例如：

（1）spy /spaɪ/ 清辅音浊化后读作 /sbaɪ/

（2）spoon /spuːn/ 清辅音浊化后读作 /sbuːn/

（3）star /staː/ 清辅音浊化后读作 /sdaː/

（4）sky /skaɪ/ 清辅音浊化后读作 /sgaɪ/

知识拓展：热词读音小知识

"莫吉托"这款鸡尾酒（见图 1-3）起源于古巴，而古巴的官方语言是西班牙语。西班牙语中"j"的发音是"h"，所以 Mojito 的正确读音是 /moʊˈhidoʊ/，但是很大部分人都把这款酒的发音读错了。

日常生活中还有许多我们会常常用到，但是又经常读错的单词。

图 1-3

（1）VS 不读 "/veɪes/"，在两人之间对决的时候我们常会用到 VS，是 VERSUS 的简写，versus 源于拉丁文，本意为"相对照，相对立"的意思，正确读音应该是 /ˈvɜːsəs/。

（2）APP 不叫 "[eɪpiːpi]"，全称是 APPLICATION，正确的读音是 /æp/。

（3）GIF 不念 "[dʒiːəɪef]"，指表情包，GIF 正确的发音应该是 /gif/。

任务实践

（1）简述英语语音的基础知识。

（2）简述英语话语表达的基本规则。

（3）失爆练习。

The girl in the re(d) coat was on a bla(ck) bike jus(t) now.

The bi(g) bus from the fa(c)tory is full of people.

This is an ol(d) pi(c)ture of a bi(g) car.

The ol(d) do(c)tor has a ca(t), too.

What would you like, ho(t) tea or bla(ck) coffee?

（4）根据本任务所学内容方法，熟练朗读下段英语广播词，正确标示出重音的符号，并使用正确的节奏和语调。

➡ Landing at a Transit Station ⬅

Ladies and gentlemen,

We have landed at _____ airport. The local time is _____. The ground temperature is 20 degrees centigrade or 68 degrees Fahrenheit. Please remain in your seats until the fasten seat belt sign is off. Please be careful when opening the overhead lockers.

Passengers to _____ please take your passport and your belongings with you when you disembark. Please get your boarding pass checked when get off the aircraft.

任务三 中英文数字的互译及度量单位

任务导入

在客舱广播时，常常会出现温度、时间、日期等数字，尤其在短途航班中供餐流程结束后就要预报落地前广播，这个时候就需要考验广播员过硬的中英文数字、度量换算基本功了。

任务要求

通过对本任务的学习，学习者应掌握各种数字及度量在广播中的转换方法。

一、中英文数字互译

(一)中英文数字互译

中文数字到万位以上,倾向于四个零做一次转换,而英文数字在书写的时候是三个零用一个逗号标注开。为了熟练进行中英文数字换算,可以牢记四个换算公式,如表1-12所示。

表 1-12 换算公式

公式1	一万 = 10 thousand
公式2	一千万 = 10 million
公式3	一亿 = 100 million
公式4	十亿 = 1 billion

(1)十七万用英语怎么表达?

参照公式1:一万是10 thousand,十七万是一万的17倍,是170 thousand。

(2)两千八百万用英语怎么表达?

参照公式2:一千万是10 million,两千八百万是28 million。

(3)七亿六千万用英语怎么表达?

参照公式3:一亿是100 million,七亿是700 million,一千万是10 million,六千万是60 million,七亿六千万就是760 million。

(4)二十五亿用英语怎么表达?

参照公式4:十亿是1 billion,二十五亿是2.5 billion。

(二)中英文分数、小数、百分数的转换

1. 分数

汉语中的分数翻译成英语的分子使用基数词,分母必用序数词。特殊的分数也有特定的表达方式。例如:

(1)1/3 英语表达为 one-third(分母要用序数)。

(2)2/3 英语表达为 two-thirds(分子不是1时,分母序数要用复数)。

(3)1/2 英语表达为 a/one half。

(4)3/4 英语表达为 three quarters。

(5)19/243 英语表达为 nineteen over two hundred and forty-three(太长的分数,用介词 over 隔开)。

2. 小数

小数的表达如下。

3.268 英文表达为 three point two six eight。小数点用"point",小数后每位数要分别读。

0.36 英文表达为 (zero) point three six。小数点前的数字若为"0"略去不读,但是正式广播中建议保留"zero"。

3. 百分数

百分数的表达如下。

50% 英文表达为 fifty percent。

12.09% 英文表达为 twelve point zero nine percent。

0.5% 英文表达为 (zero) point five percent（正式广播中应保留 zero）。

（三）中英文月份、日期、节日对照

中英文中的月份、日期对照如表 1-13~ 表 1-15 所示。

表 1-13　中英文月份转换

一月	January	七月	July
二月	February	八月	August
三月	March	九月	September
四月	April	十月	October
五月	May	十一月	November
六月	June	十二月	December

表 1-14　中英文日期转换

1月1日	January the first	the 1st of January
2月2日	February the second	the 2nd of February
3月3日	March the third	the 3rd of March
4月4日	April the forth	the 4th of April
5月8日	May the eighth	the 8th of May
6月21日	June the twenty-first	the 21st of June
7月24日	July the twenty-forth	the 24th of July
8月25日	August the twenty-fifth	the 25th of August
9月10日	September the tenth	the 10th of September
12月31日	December the thirty-first	the 31st of December
农历十二月二十九	December the 29th of Chinese Lunar Calendar/year	
农历正月初一	January the 1st of Chinese Lunar Calendar/year	
农历正月十五	the fifteenth day of the first lunar month	
五月的第二个星期日	the second Sunday of May	

表 1-15　中英文节日表述

元旦	New Year's Day
除夕	Spring Festival Eve/Chinese New Year's Eve
春节	Spring Festival
元宵节	(Chinese) Lantern Festival
端午节	Dragon Boat Festival
建军节	Army Day
教师节	Teacher's Day
中秋节	Mid-Autumn Festival
国庆节	National Day
重阳节	Double Ninth Day
平安夜	Christmas Eve
圣诞节	Christmas Day

二、中英文时间、度量单位等的转换

（一）中英文时间等转换

时间单位的中英文如表 1-16 所示。

表 1-16　时间单位

秒	second
分钟	minute
一刻钟	quarter
小时	hour
早上	in the morning/a.m.
中午	at noon
下午	in the afternoon/p.m.
傍晚	at night
夜晚	in the evening
午夜	(at) midnight
今晚	tonight

具体时间的中英文表达如表 1-17 所示（中文播报时一般国内入港航班在时间前加上北京时间，国际出港航班在时间前加上当地时间）。

表 1-17　具体时间的中英文表达

0:00	凌晨 0 点	twelve midnight/zero a.m.
0:30	凌晨 0 点 30 分	thirty past twelve in the morning/zero thirty a.m.
9:10	早上 9 点 10 分	ten past nine in the morning/nine ten a.m.
10:00	早上 10 点	ten o'clock in the morning/ten a.m.
12:00	中午 12 点（整）	twelve o'clock at noon/twelve p.m.
12:15	中午 12 点 15 分	a quarter past twelve in the afternoon/twelve fifteen p.m.
15:20	下午 3 点 20 分	twenty past three in the afternoon/three twenty p.m.
18:55	晚上 6 点 55 分	five to seven at night/six fifty-five p.m.
20:45	晚上 8 点 45 分	a quarter to nine in the evening/eight forty-five p.m.

年份的中英文表达如表 1-18 所示。

表 1-18　年份

1998	nineteen ninety-eight
2000	(year) two thousand
2009	two thousand and nine
2017	two thousand and seventeen/twenty seventeen
2020	two thousand and twenty/twenty twenty

（二）度量及其他的中英文表述

距离的中英文表达如表 1-19 所示。

表 1-19　距离

1180km	1180 千米	one thousand one hundred and eighty kilometers
8080km	8080 千米	eight thousand and eighty kilometers
1506km	1506 千米	one thousand five hundred and six kilometers

温度的中英文表达如表 1-20 所示。其中，华氏温标用 Fahrenheit/ˈfærəhaɪt/ 表达，符号为 ℉，摄氏温标的英文为 Celsius/ˈselsiəs/ 或 Centigrade/ˈsentigreid/，符号为 ℃。

表 1-20　温度

73.4 摄氏度	seventy-three point four degrees Celsius/Centigrade (/ˈsentɪgreɪd/)
0.4℃	zero point four degrees Celsius/Centigrade
−75 华氏度	minus seventy-five degrees Fahrenheit
−0.6℉	minus (zero) point six degrees Fahrenheit

航班号的英文表达如表 1-21 所示。

表 1-21　航班号

CZ301	CZ three zero/O one
MU327	MU three two seven
CA6501	CA six five zero/O one
KL610	KL six one zero/O

机型的英文表达如表 1-22 所示。

表 1-22　机型

A330-300	Airbus three thirty three hundred
空客 380	Airbus three eighty
B737	Boeing seven three seven
波音 777-200	Boeing triple seven two hundred

知识拓展：客机型号的渊源

1. 波音飞机

第二次世界大战后，波音公司将业务扩展到民用飞机以及导弹和航天飞机等新领域。工程部门开始以 100 为单位为新产品领域划分型号，例如 300 和 400 继续代表飞机产品，500 用于代表涡轮发动机产品，600 用于火箭和导弹，700 则用于运输飞机。然而营销部门认为首款民用喷气机用"700 型"并不容易被人记住，因此跳过几个数字直接叫"707 型"，因为这个名字中的"7"有重复，更容易被人记住的，专门用于民用喷气机。从最初的 717 命名开始，所有的波音民用喷气机都在 7X7 这一格式的基础上命名，分别称为 727、737、747、787。

2. 空客飞机

1969 年，空客公司开始研制的第一款机型是 A300，这是世界上第一款双发宽体客机，由于其设计载客能力是 300 人，且其公司首字母是 A，所以称为 A300。后来空客在 A300 的基础上又开发了 A310，此后便形成惯例，所有的客机均以 A3X0 命名，如 A320、A330、A340、A380、A350。

3. C919飞机（见图1-4）

C是China的首字母，也是商飞英文COMAC的首字母，第一个"9"的寓意是天长地久，"19"代表的是中国首型中型客机最大载客量为190人。同时"C"还寓意立志要跻身国际大型客机市场，要与Airbus（空客）和Boeing（波音）一道在国际宽体大型客机制造业中形成ABC并立的格局。

图 1-4

任务实践

（1）列举中英文数字进制换算四个公式。

（2）背诵、默写出摄氏度、华氏度的三种英文表述。

（3）根据本任务所学的各种中英文表述，补充完整下段广播词，并流利地朗读。

▶ 国内航班落地广播（节选）◀

女士们，先生们：

我们已经到达_____机场，现在是_____（北京/当地）时间_____点_____分，地面温度_____摄氏度，_____华氏度。

Ladies and Gentlemen,

We have just arrived at _____ airport, the local time is _____. The ground temperature is _____ degrees Celsius/Centigrade or _____ degrees Fahrenheit.

任务四　民航乘务员客舱广播技巧及注意事项

任务导入

客舱广播是指服务过程中，乘务员借助一定的词汇、语气、语调广播与乘客进行交流的一种比较规范的沟通方式。其内容主要涉及飞行航程、飞行概况、航线地理、航段介绍、空中服务等方面。绝大部分的机上广播具有语言柔和、清晰、纯正等特点。

任务要求

通过本任务的学习，学习者应掌握基本客舱广播的技巧。

一、客舱广播基本原则

（一）广播执行者

客舱广播的执行者分为两类。

（1）乘务长根据人员信息，指定具有广播员资格的乘务员进行广播。

（2）机上预录广播。预录广播一般用于航空公司规定的迎客、送客、安全须知以及乘务员繁忙服务等阶段，或者颠簸、滑行时也选用预录广播。

（二）广播语言顺序

1. 国内航空公司

在国内航班中，广播顺序为中文—英文。

在国际航班中的广播顺序为中文—英文—目的地国家语言。

2. 其他国家国际航空公司

如果该航班属于国际航空公司，则应按照航空公司所有国语言—目的地语言—根据当天航班乘客国籍情况和乘务员国籍情况增加一种语言广播的顺序广播。

（三）广播内容

航空公司会提供常规广播词。一般广播词中括号的内容为可选项，广播员可根据航班实际情况决定是否播读；广播词中标有 A、B、C 等序号的内容为根据不同机型、不同航线、不同舱位制定的同一广播项的不同选项，广播员可根据当天航班的实际情况自行选择进行播读。

（四）广播要求

（1）基本要求：语速适中、咬字清晰。

（2）服务类广播词：语气亲切、自然。

（3）紧急情况广播词：语气坚定、沉稳。

（4）总体要求：客舱广播应该在最短的时间用最简洁的语言、用最快的速度把真实的信息传播出去。客舱广播不是念稿子，字里行间渗透着乘务员对内容的理解，并把这种理解、感受真切地传达给乘客，因此要做到以下 4 点。

① 准确无误，即时间、地点、人物、事件、原因、结果都要准确无误。

② 层次清晰，即导语、主体、结尾、层次之间要留出停顿时间，以免播成一段。

③ 节奏明快，即注意节奏的快慢，句子与句子之间紧凑，段落之间明白通畅。

④ 朴实大气，即正常情况下的广播就是叙述事件，不做任何夸张、渲染。

二、客舱广播技巧

（一）内部技巧

客航广播的内部技巧主要是指空中乘务人员良好的心理素质、灵活的应变能力以及与乘客之间的情感交流。

1. 乘务员的心理素质

飞机在飞行时受内外多种因素的影响，容易出现一系列的突发状况，如果乘务员在遇到这类意外状况时不能冷静沉着地做出反应，其后续工作将无法顺利开展。因此，空中乘务人员需要拥有良好的心理素质，冷静沉着应对，并作出正确的操作。

2. 乘务员的应变能力

如果飞行过程中出现突发状况，乘客会出现不同程度的慌张、紧张、焦急等情绪，此时需要乘务员针对突发状况作出积极、正确的解答，在播报过程应保证语言简洁、逻辑清晰、语气平和，在第一时间做好乘客的心理安抚工作。如果乘务员缺乏良好的应变能力，客舱广播不仅无法发挥其应有的作用，反而会带来一定的负面影响。

3. 乘务员的情感交流能力

在航班播报的过程，乘务员利用话筒完成信息的播报任务能拉近乘务员与乘客之间的距离，将乘客真正关注的内容通过客舱广播的形式传达给乘客。

（二）外部技巧

客舱广播的外部技巧主要体现在空中乘务人员的发音、语气、语速、重音 4 个方面。

1. 发音的规范性

语言是人际交往的基本手段，能够影响到他人对自己的第一印象。在客舱广播的过程中，如果乘务员在发音上存在一定的缺陷，乘客在收听时，可能对客舱广播内容出现认知性偏差，甚至错过一些重要信息，严重降低客舱广播的应用质量，降低乘客对空中服务的满意度。因此，我国民航要求每一位空中乘务员均能够使用规范的普通话和英语，并将此作为乘务员取得广播员资格的基本标准。

2. 语气的准确性

客舱广播的语气是指乘务员在某种特定情感下所展现出来的一种声音形式，乘务员在开展客舱广播时，应积极控制好个人情绪，用稳定、平和的心态应对飞行过程遇到的各种突发情况；用热情、饱满的态度为乘客提供广播服务。在播报信息时，乘务员应保证语气平缓，口腔自然放松，把握好抑扬顿挫。

3. 语速的适宜性

在客舱广播的过程，乘务员播报信息的语速过快或过慢均会给乘客带来不适感，每一段信息播报均要保持语速适中。紧急情况下更需要乘务员尽快调整好语速，在播报处理时可适当提升语速，同时不可因紧张导致语速过快，避免给乘客带来慌乱、紧张的感觉。

4. 重音的科学性

客舱广播中若要将信息的层次关系与轻重关系向乘客传达出来，就需要乘务员在播报信息的过程正确把握播报内容、突出情感表达、强化语义、丰富语言色彩，全面处理好重音。信息播报过程中，若信息中的数字或文字频繁重复出现，需要根据其所在的语境及重要性进行判断，明确哪些信息需要使用重音进行强调、哪些则无须强调。

（三）信息播报的技巧

信息播报的技巧包括以下 4 点。

1. 态度把握技巧

在广播的过程中，虽然有引导性的内容，但也需要乘务员把事实叙述清楚，让乘客去理解、感受，这就意味着广播的态度要控制分寸，不能采用命令的方式。

2. 长句处理技巧

有时客舱广播词为了叙述的连贯性或者表达的明确性，也会有长句，这就要求乘务员应将句子的语法关系、逻辑关系表达清楚，使乘客一听就明白。

（1）要处理好停连，避免语意含混。为了使长句的语意清楚又连贯，常用声断气连，即似停非停似连非连的方法，以语流的细微变化来表现语句关系。

（2）要精选重音，以免由于重音过多而使听众的注意力分散，破坏了节奏的明快感，还可以节省气息，使语流通畅自如。

（3）要注意语势的承上启下，加大语流的起伏变化，突出语句目的。

3. 数字处理技巧

读准、读清是数字处理的基本要求。数字信息能够对乘客起到提示的作用，便于了解数字真正的含义。如果数字较多，就要精选有价值的、最直观的数字重音，这样才使客舱广播的表达重点突出，简洁明快。

4. 广播速度技巧

停连要符合乘客心理的需要，有时候听明白内容需要一定的时间，如果语速太快，不仅让听的人反应不过来，还会使广播者的语音与思维脱节。因此可以用语气的转折和起伏区分层次，突出重点，加强对比，引起乘客的注意才能广播内容完全被接收。乘务员还要利用语流的疏密变化，加大层间和语句内的主次对比，展开主要的，带过次要的。

三、客舱广播注意事项

（一）与航空心理对接

与航空心理对接是特殊航空运输的核心内容，也是加强客舱广播服务建设的必要措施。

1. 广播时与乘客心理波动时机对接

飞机起飞之前在转场过程中乘客心理既激动兴奋又有些紧张，此时客舱广播可以向乘客讲述飞机即将起飞的过程，并提醒乘客做好相应的安全措施。

2. 服务信心的建立

在飞行过程中，有的乘客心情特别放松，有的乘客会一直紧张，此时客舱广播可以通过播放轻音乐或介绍航线地理内容等使乘客对航空公司和机上服务建立起信任。

3. 传递飞行安全知识

飞机颠簸时，提醒乘客收起小桌板并系好安全带；起飞和降落时为防止高空飞行对耳膜的损害，可以提醒乘客进行咀嚼动作等。客舱广播良好的时机选择，能够使乘客始终感受到贴心的服务，并且在乘客最需要鼓励的时候，能够获得最及时的信息支持。

（二）与旅程文化对接

与旅程文化的对接是展示企业文化特色和航空旅行特色的主要方式。飞行过程中，乘客不能使用手机，不能收听收音机，所以绝大多数乘客尤其是经济舱乘客娱乐信息来源就是客舱广播，乘客除了休息、用餐、办公外会静心收听广播内容，此时正是航空公司传播企业文化信息的好时机。此外，航空旅行文化通常还包括地理区域文化和航空专业文化，客舱广播中如果适当增加这些内容必定会增加航空旅行的满意度，舒缓乘客的紧张情绪，增加乘客的航空知识。这些也都是广播员在特色广播中需要注意的事项。

（三）以动态乘客为中心

每次航班的乘客都不会相同，因此客舱广播的受众流动性大，潜在客户也多，如果对每一批流动客户都能进行有效的客舱广播，既能增大航空公司的知名度，又能通过口碑吸引更多的客户。所以航空公司要抓住乘客先入为主的特点，以优质广播服务和完善信息内容向乘客传递航空企业价值，从产品信息传达的角度提升乘客对航空服务的价值认识和安全认识，促进乘客二次消费。而承担广播工作的乘务员就是良好的媒介。

知识拓展：机长广播让乘客更有"安全感"

对于首次乘机的乘客来说，如何使他们放松紧张的心情，机长广播往往比乘务员广播更具有说服力，更能带给乘客更多的安心。因此，近年来，机长广播已频繁地出现在客舱内，一般机长广播平飞后进行。在航班延误或飞机出现颠簸时，机长广播更会让乘客安静下来，机长掌握着空中航路情况，此时机长广播作一个简单的介绍或解释，往往会收到事半功倍的效果（见图1-5）。

图 1-5

任务实践

（1）简述客舱广播的基本原则。
（2）简述客舱广播的注意事项。

（3）根据本任务所学内容及方法，熟练朗读下段中英文广播词，注意正确使用广播技巧。

> 发放乘客意见卡广播词

女士们，先生们：

欢迎您乘坐_____航空公司航班，为了帮助我们不断提高服务质量，敬请留下宝贵意见，谢谢您的关心与支持！

Ladies and Gentlemen,

　　Welcome aboard _____ Airlines. Your comments will be highly valued in order to improve our service.

　　Thank you for your support.

（注：这类广播的目的是征求意见，要说明目的、请求，语气要诚恳。）

本项目教学音频

项目二
民航机场与航班广播常识

项目目标

知识目标	掌握国际国内主要机场三字代码； 了解航线地标的组成、读法和作用； 掌握华氏与摄氏温度换算表及换算法； 了解各国入境海关检疫规定。
技能目标	由三字代码熟练辨认出国际国内主要机场； 流利专业地进行航线地标的播读； 熟练进行华氏与摄氏温度换算； 能够讲出各国最主要的入境海关检疫规定。
职业素养目标	培养学生爱岗敬业的精神； 培养学生机上广播职业素养； 培养学生对旅客的主动服务意识； 培养学生精益求精的工匠精神。

任务一　机场三字代码

任务导入

机场三字代码简称"三字代码"，由国际航空运输协会（International Air Transport Association，IATA）制定。国际航空运输协会对世界上的国家、城市、机场以及加入国际航空运输协会的航空公司制定了统一的编码。在空运中，以三个英文字母简写航空机场名。本任务以三字代码为主线，将对客舱广播时所涉及的机场、航空公司代码等进行简单介绍。

任务要求

通过对本任务的学习，学习者应了解并能够识别各地机场三字代码和各大航空公司代码，新聘乘务员应能背诵出至少20个主要城市的三字代码。

一、国内部分机场名称及三字代码

国内部分机场名称及三字代码见表2-1。

表2-1 国内部分机场名称及三字代码

地区	城市	机场名称	三字代码	地区	城市	机场名称	三字代码
北京	北京	首都	PEK	浙江	义乌	义乌	YIW
		大兴	PKX		衢州	衢州	JUZ
上海	上海	虹桥	SHA		舟山	朱家尖	HSN
		浦东	PVG	安徽	合肥	新桥	HFE
天津	天津	滨海	TSN		黄山	屯溪	TXN
重庆	重庆	江北	CKG		安庆	天柱山	AQG
河北	石家庄	正定	SJW	福建	福州	长乐	FOC
	秦皇岛	山海关	SHP		厦门	高崎	XMN
山西	太原	武宿	TYN		泉州	晋江	JJN
	长治	长治	CIH		武夷山	武夷山	WUS
	运城	张孝	YCU	江西	南昌	昌北	KHN
内蒙古	呼和浩特	白塔	HET		九江	庐山	JIU
	包头	包头	BAV		赣州	黄金	KOW
	海拉尔	东山	HLD		景德镇	罗家	JDZ
	锡林浩特	锡林浩特	XIL	广东	广州	白云	CAN
吉林	长春	龙嘉	CGQ		深圳	宝安	SZX
	吉林	二台子	JIL		湛江	湛江	ZHA
	延吉	朝阳川	YNJ		珠海	金湾	ZUH
辽宁	沈阳	仙桃	SHE		梅县	梅县	MXZ
	大连	周水子	DLC		汕头	外砂	SWA
	丹东	浪头	DDG	湖南	长沙	黄花	CSX
	锦州	锦州湾	JNZ		常德	桃花源	CDG
	朝阳	朝阳	CHG		张家界	荷花	DYG
黑龙江	哈尔滨	太平	HRB		衡阳	南岳	HNY
	齐齐哈尔	三家子	NDG	山东	济南	遥墙	TNA
	佳木斯	东郊	JMU		青岛	胶东	TAO
	牡丹江	海浪	MDG		烟台	蓬莱	YNT
河南	郑州	新郑	CGO		潍坊	潍坊	WEF
	洛阳	洛阳	LYA		威海	威海	WEH
	南阳	姜营	NNY		临沂	启阳	LYI
浙江	杭州	萧山	HGH		济宁	曲阜	JNG
	宁波	栎社	NGB	云南	昆明	长水	KMG
	温州	龙湾	WNZ		景洪	西双版纳嘎洒	JHG
	黄岩	路桥	HYN		丽江	三义	LJG

续表

地 区	城 市	机场名称	三字代码	地 区	城 市	机场名称	三字代码
云南	大理	大理	DLU	贵州	贵阳	龙洞堡	KWE
	芒市	芒市	LUM		铜仁	凤凰	TEN
	香格里拉	迪庆香格里拉	DIG	四川	成都	双流	CYU
西藏	拉萨	贡嘎	LXA		泸州	云龙	LZO
陕西	西安	咸阳	SIA		宜宾	宜宾	YBP
	汉中	汉中	HZG		广元	盘龙	GYS
	延安	延安	ENY		绵阳	南郊	MIG
新疆	乌鲁木齐	地窝堡	URC		西昌	青山	XIC
	伊宁	伊宁	YIN		九寨沟	黄龙	JZH
	喀什	喀什	KHG	甘肃	兰州	中川	LHW
	库尔勒	库尔勒	KRL		敦煌	敦煌	DNH
	阿克苏	阿克苏	AKU	广西	南宁	吴圩	NNG
	阿勒泰	阿勒泰	AAT		桂林	两江	KWL
	和田	和田	HTN		柳州	白莲	LZH
	库车	库车	KCA		北海	福成	BHY
	且末	且末	IQN		梧州	长洲岛	WUZ
	塔城	塔城	TCG	江苏	常州	牵牛	CZX
海南	海口	美兰	HAK		徐州	观音	XUE
	三亚	凤凰	SYX		连云港	白塔埠	LYG
湖北	武汉	天河	WUH		南通	兴东	NTG
	襄樊	刘集	XFN		盐城	南洋	YNZ
	荆州	沙市	SHS		无锡	硕放	WUX
	宜昌	三峡	YIH		南京	禄口	NKG
	恩施	恩施	ENH	宁夏	银川	河东	INC

二、国内机场三字代码速记法

一般国内航空公司要求乘务员主要记忆国内机场的三字代码，而国际城市三字代码主要就是根据英文来记忆的，所以本任务对国际航空机场的三字代码的记忆方法不做特别介绍。国内机场三字代码大多根据拼音生成，所以大多数可以在拼音的基础上记忆。

（一）三字城市名称速记

三个字的城市名，代码刚好是其拼音的首字母的情况最为好记。如连云港 LYG、景德镇 JDZ、吉安 JGS（井冈山机场）等。这种情况也存在变化记忆，如城市名含有"尔"字，以 R 来代替"尔"，常见的有哈尔滨 HRB、库尔勒 KRL 等。

（二）直接记名法

直接取城市名拼音前三个字母的，例如武汉 WUH、吉林 JIL、沈阳 SHE、上海 SHA、大同 DAT、九江 JIU、义乌 YIW、湛江 ZHA、无锡 WUX 等。

（三）两字首拼记忆法（Ⅰ）

两个字的城市名大多取两个字的拼音首字母再加其中一个字拼音的某一个字母。

（1）拼音中以 N 或 G 结尾的，经常取 N 或 G。取第一个字结尾的有：温州 WNZ、延吉 YNJ、锦州 JNZ、南阳 NNY、烟台 YNT、常德 CGD、宁波 NGB、敦煌 DNH 等；取第二个字结尾的有：富蕴 FYN、丹东 DDG、安阳 AYN、太原 TYN、襄樊 XFN、黄岩 HYN、南通 NTG、厦门 XMN、广汉 GHN、汉中 HZG、嘉峪关 JGN（"嘉关"）、昆明 KMG、济宁 JNG、丽江 LJG、西双版纳 JHG（景洪机场）、南宁 NNG、和田 HTN、塔城 TCG、安庆 AQG、张家界 DYG（张家界又名大庸）等。

（2）不取 N 或 G 的，经常取某一个字的第一个元音字母。取第一个字第一个元音字母的机场如海口 HAK、威海 WEH、东营 DOY、潍坊 WEF、昭通 ZAT、珠海 ZUH、赤峰 CIF、武夷山 WUS（"武山"）等。

（3）取第二个字第一个元音的机场如佳木斯 JMU、洛阳 LYA、临沂 LYI、合肥 HFE、遵义 ZYI、安康 AKA、库车 KCA、哈密 HMI、泸州 LZO、攀枝花 PZI。

（4）部分拼音声母有 H 的，取两个首字母加 H，如沙市 SHS、韶关 SHG、九寨沟 JZH、柳州 LZH 等。

（四）两字首拼记忆法（Ⅱ）

取两个字拼音的首字母，后面跟一个与城市名拼音无关的字母，如大连 DLC、秦皇岛 SHP（山海关机场）、石家庄 SJW、运城 YCU、长沙 CSX、黄山 TXN（屯溪机场）、常州 CZX、梅县 MXZ、深圳 SZX、三亚 SYX、宜宾 YBP、广元 GYS、大理 DLU、保山 BSD（联想到云端机场，就会记住 D）、鄂尔多斯 DSN（重点在多斯）、海拉尔 HLD、锡林浩特 XTL（联想成锡特林）、林芝 LZY、北海 BHY 等。

（五）无规律拼音记忆法

与拼音有关，无统一规律的，如黑河 HEK（可以当作谐音读，注意跟海口 HAK 区分）、恩施 ENH、宜昌 YIH、衡阳 HNY、阜阳 FUG、杭州 HGH、衢州 JUZ（联想方言读"菊州"）、盐城 YNZ（谐音"严整"）、晋江 JJN、绵阳 MIG、达州 DAX、南充 NAO（联想这里很闹）、西宁 XNN、文山 WNH、临沧 LNJ、思茅 SYM、梧州 YUZ、包头 BAV、乌兰浩特 HLH（联想是呼兰浩特）、通辽 TGO、乌海 WUA、阿勒泰 AAT、阿克苏 AKU、且末 IQM 等。

（六）首拼音字母记忆法

取城市名拼音的第一个字母，后面跟两个与拼音无关的字母，如鞍山 AOG（可以联想鞍钢，就会记住 G）、长春 CGQ（可以跟郑州 CGO 放在一起记）、潮阳 CHG、长海 CNI、兴城 XEN、长治 CIH、怀化 HJJ、泗水 SUB、汕头 SWA、万州 WXN、西昌 XTC、铜仁 TEN、安顺 AVA、兰州 LHW、格尔木 GOQ、上海（浦东）PVG、喀什 KHG 等。

（七）城市名称谐音法

跟城市英文名或者方言、谐音有关，如北京（首都机场）PEK（北京的英文名字也用 Peking）、南京 NKG（Nanking）、乌鲁木齐 URC（Urumchi，也作 Urumqi）、广州 CAN（Canton，粤语"广州"的音译）、呼和浩特 HET（Huhhot，用谐音"和特"来记）、青岛（Tsingtao）、西安（西关机场）SIA（Sian）、天津 TSN（Tientsin）、福州 FOC（Foochow）、桂林 KWL（Kweilin）、重庆 CKG（Chungking）、成都 CTU、延安 ENY（谐音）、拉萨 LXA、克拉玛依 KRY、赣州 KOW 等。

三、部分国际城市三字代码

部分国际城市三字代码如表 2-2 所示。

表 2-2 部分国际城市三字代码

中文名称	英文名称	三字代码	中文名称	英文名称	三字代码
阿姆斯特丹	Amsterdam	AMS	法兰克福	Frankfurt	FRA
奥克兰	Auckland	AKL	福冈	Fukuoka	FUK
巴林	Bahrain	BAH	日内瓦	Geneva	CVA
曼谷	Bangkok	BKK	汉堡	Hamburg	HAM
巴塞罗那	Barcelona	BCN	河内	Hanoi	HAN
柏林	Berlin	BER	赫尔辛基	Helsinki	HEL
孟买	Bombay	BOM	广岛	Hiroshima	HIJ
波士顿	Boston	BOS	胡志明	Ho Chi Minh	SCN
布里斯班	Brisbane	BNE	雅加达	Jakarta	JKT
布鲁塞尔	Brussels	BRU	卡拉奇	Karachi	KHI
开罗	Cairo	CAI	拉斯维加斯	Las Vegas	LAS
哥本哈根	Copenhagen	CPH	伦敦	London	LHR
德里	Delhi	DEL	洛杉矶	Los Angeles	LAX
迪拜	Dubai	DXB	卢森堡	Luxembourg	LUX

续表

中文名称	英文名称	三字代码	中文名称	英文名称	三字代码
曼彻斯特	Manchester	MAN	釜山	Pusan	PUS
马尼拉	Manila	MNL	罗马	Rome	ROM
墨尔本	Melbourne	MEL	旧金山	San Francisca	SEO
墨西哥城	Mexico City	MEX	圣地亚哥	Santiago	SCI
慕尼黑	Munich	MUC	札幌	Sapporo	SPK
长崎	Nagasaki	NGS	西雅图	Seattle	SEA
名古屋	Nagoya	NCO	首尔	Seoul	SEL
纽约	New York	NYC	新加坡	Singapore	SIN
奥克兰	Oakland Ca	OAK	悉尼	Sydney	SYD
大阪	Osaka	OSA	东京	Tokyo	TYO
巴黎	Paris	CDG	温哥华	Vancouver	YVR
金边	Phnom Penh	PNH	华盛顿	Washington	WAS

四、部分航空公司二字代码

（一）国内航空代码

国内航空代码见表 2-3。

表 2-3　国内航空代码

公司标识	二字代码	中文名称	英文简称
	CA	中国国际航空股份有限公司	Air China
	MU	中国东方航空股份有限公司	China Eastern Airlines
	CZ	中国南方航空股份有限公司	China Southern Airlines
	HU	海南航空股份有限公司	Hainan Airlines
	FM	上海航空股份有限公司	Shanghai Airlines
	SC	山东航空股份有限公司	Shandong Airlines
	ZH	深圳航空有限责任公司	Shenzhen Airlines

续表

公司标识	二字代码	中文名称	英文简称
	3U	四川航空股份有限公司	Sichuan Airlines
	MF	厦门航空有限公司	Xiamen Airlines
	CX	国泰航空有限公司	Cathay Pacific Airways
	NX	澳门航空股份有限公司	Air Macau

（二）国际航空代码

国际航空代码见表 2-4。

表 2-4　国际航空代码

公司标识	二字代码	中文名称	英文简称
KOREAN AIR	KE	大韩航空公司	Korean Air Lines
Asiana Airlines	OZ	韩亚航空公司	Asiana Airlines
JAL	JL	日本航空公司	Japan Airlines
ANA	NH	全日空公司	All Nippon Airways
SINGAPORE AIRLINES	SQ	新加坡航空公司	Singapore Airlines
THAI	TG	泰国国际航空公司	Thai Airways International
NORTHWEST AIRLINES	NW	美国西北航空公司	Northwest Airlines
AIR CANADA	AC	加拿大国际航空公司	Canadian Airlines International

续表

公司标识	二字代码	中文名称	英文简称
	UA	美国联合航空公司	United Airlines
	BA	英国航空公司	British Airways
	KL	荷兰皇家航空公司	KIM Royal Dutch Airlines
	LH	德国汉莎航空公司	Lufthansa
	AF	法国航空公司	Air France
	OS	奥地利航空公司	Austrian Airlines AG
	SU	俄罗斯国际航空公司	Aeroflot-Russian Airlines
	QF	澳洲航空公司	Qantas Airways
	AY	芬兰航空公司	Finn Air
	AZ	意大利航空公司	Alitalia
	SK	斯堪的纳维亚（北欧）航空公司	Scandinavian Airlines Systems
	BI	文莱皇家航空公司	Royal Brunei Airlines
	GA	印度尼西亚鹰航空公司	Garuda Indonesia
	MH	马来西亚航空公司	Malaysian Airlines System Berhad
	PR	菲律宾航空公司	Philippine Airlines
	VN	越南航空公司	Vietnam Airlines
	EK	阿拉伯联合酋长国航空公司（阿联酋航空）	Emirates Airways

知识拓展：航班号小知识

为了方便运输和用户查询，每个航班均编有航班号。

我国国际航班的编号由执行该航班任务的航空公司的二字代码和三个阿拉伯数字组成，其中最后一个数字为奇数表示去程航班，最后一个数字为偶数表示回程航班。如CA982指中国国际航空公司承担的自纽约返回北京的国际航班。

我国国内航班的航班号由执行航班任务的航空公司二字代码和四个阿拉伯数字组成，其中第一位数字表示执行该航班任务的航空公司或所属管理局，第二位数字表示该航班终点站所属的管理局，第三、四位数字表示班次，即该航班的具体编号，其中第四位数字若为奇数表示该航班为去程航班；偶数表示回程航班。例如CA1201表示由中国国际航空公司担任的由北京至西安的去程航班；MU5302是指东方航空公司担任的由长沙至上海的回程航班。

任务实践

（1）背诵国内机场三字代码表。
（2）根据本任务所学内容填写表2-5。

表2-5 课后习题

昆明	长水	
恩施		ENH
MU	中国东方航空股份有限公司	
		Air Macau

任务二　航线地标

任务导入

航空专业学生所学的航线地理，包括国内内地主要航线、国内港澳台地区航线、国际主要航线，是从主要航空港、主要城市及其旅游资源两方面进行学习，而本任务所涉及的客舱广播中的"航线地标"包括国内和国际主要航线的飞行距离、沿线地标、国家、省份等。在实际飞行中，乘务员不但要播报航线信息，有时乘客会询问飞行中的地点，这也是考验乘务员航线地标的知识。

任务要求

通过本任务的学习，读者应能看懂和识别航线地标各类信息，并能够在广播中灵活运用。

一、国内部分机场信息

国内部分机场信息见表2-6。

表2-6　国内部分机场信息

机场名称	方位	离城距离/千米
北京首都国际机场	东北	25.4
上海虹桥国际机场	西南	13
上海浦东国际机场	东南	32.3
广州白云国际机场	西北	28
深圳宝安国际机场	西北	32
杭州萧山国际机场	东北	27
厦门高崎国际机场	东南	10
武汉天河国际机场	西北	25
成都双流国际机场	西南	16
南京禄口国际机场	正南	35.8
长沙黄花国际机场	正南	23.5
青岛胶东国际机场	西北	39

续表

机场名称	方位	离城距离/千米
西安咸阳国际机场	东北	25
大连周水子国际机场	西北	9.5
桂林两江国际机场	西南	28
重庆江北国际机场	东北	19
哈尔滨太平国际机场	西南	33
福州长乐国际机场	东南	39.2
昆明长水国际机场	东北	24.5
北海福成机场	东北	24
舟山普陀山机场	西北	17.6
三亚凤凰国际机场	西北	11
郑州新郑国际机场	东南	29.5
海口美兰国际机场	东南	18

注：了解机场的离城距离可以帮助乘客安排去机场或下机后的路线并计算路程大致所需时间。

二、国外部分机场信息

国外部分机场信息见表 2-7。

表 2-7 国外部分机场信息

机场名称	方位	离城距离/千米
仁川国际机场	西南	23.5
关西国际机场	西南	35
东京国际机场	东北	17
福冈机场	正东	12
名古屋机场	正北	8
新加坡樟宜国际机场	西南	17.2
马德里巴拉哈斯国际机场	东北	12
悉尼金斯福德史密斯国际机场	西南	10
巴黎夏尔戴高乐机场	正北	25
洛杉矶国际机场	西南	19
旧金山国际机场	南	21
马尼拉国际机场	正南	10
迪拜国际机场	西南	4
吉隆坡国际机场	西南	19.5

三、国内部分航线地标

国内航线地标仅列举京沪、沪广、沪深三条最频繁的国内航线，见表2-8~表2-10。由此条京沪航线为例可以看出，同一条航线，来回程的飞行距离、时间、经过省（区市）和地标等都不完全相同，所以乘务员在客舱广播之前认真查看航线地标是很必要的准备工作。

表2-8　上海—北京—上海航线地标

机型	航段	机场名称	时差	距离	时间	地标 省（区市）	地标 城市、湖泊、河流、山脉、岛屿
双通道飞机	上海—北京（SHA-PEK）	上海虹桥国际机场 北京首都国际机场		1146km	1小时40分钟	去程：江苏省、山东省、河北省	城市：太仓—南通—邳（pī）县—济南—泊头
双通道飞机	北京—上海（PEK-SHA）	北京首都国际机场 上海虹桥国际机场		1140km	1小时30分钟	回程：河北省、山东省、江苏省	城市：石家庄—泊头—济南—邳县—无锡

表2-9　上海—广州—上海航线地标

机型	航段	机场名称	时差	距离	时间	地标 省（区市）	地标 城市、湖泊、河流、山脉、岛屿
单通道飞机	上海—广州 SHA-CAN	上海虹桥国际机场 广州白云国际机场		1235km	1小时50分钟 1小时40分钟	去程：浙江省、江西省、广东省 回程：广东省、福建省、浙江省	城市：南浔—桐庐—上饶—赣州 城市：龙门—连城—南平—东山

注："SHA"表示上海虹桥国际机场，"PVG"表示上海浦东国际机场。

表2-10　上海—深圳—上海航线地标

机型	航段	机场名称	时差	距离	时间	地标 省（区市）	地标 城市、湖泊、河流、山脉、岛屿
双通道飞机	上海—深圳 SHA-SZX	上海虹桥国际机场 深圳宝安国际机场		1303km	2小时 1小时50分钟	浙江省、福建省、广东省	去程：南浔—桐庐—云和—福州—厦门—汕头 回程：龙门—连城—南平—东山

注：机场三字代码就在航线地标上用到了，最后这项地标中如果飞行途中会经过湖泊、山脉等也会相应地标注出来，所以航线地标也是很好的旅游参考信息。

四、国际部分航线地标

（一）国际短程航线

国际短程航线见表2-11。

表2-11　上海—东京（成田）—上海航线地标

机型	航段	机场名称	时差	距离	时间	地标 国家、省（区市）	地标 城市、湖泊、河流、山脉、岛屿
单通道飞机	上海—东京（SHA-NRT）	上海虹桥国际机场		1975km	2小时15分钟	中国、日本	上海—东海—福汇岛—长崎（Nagasaki）—九州山脉—宇和岛（Uwajima）—四国（Shikoku）—幻伊水道—八剑山—伊势海湾
		成田国际机场	+1	1872km	3小时40分钟		

注：日本时间比中国早一个小时，所以"时差"项在回程显示"+1"；国际航线地标在一些重要的地名旁边会标注相应的英文。

（二）国际中程航线

国际中程航线见表2-12。

表2-12　上海—新加坡—上海标线地标

机型	航段	机场名称	时差	距离	时间	地标 国家、省（区市）	地标 城市、湖泊、河流、山脉、岛屿
双通道飞机	上海—新加坡 SHA-SIN	上海虹桥国际机场		4059km	5小时	中国（浙江省、江西省、广东省）马来西亚、新加坡	上海—南浔—桐庐—上饶—赣州—广州—香港—南海—南沙群岛—新加坡
		新加坡樟宜国际机场			4小时50分钟		

（三）国际远程航线

国际远程航线见表2-13。

表2-13　上海—悉尼—上海航线地标

机型	航段	机场名称	时差	距离	时间	地标 国家、省（区市）	地标 城市、湖泊、河流、山脉、岛屿
双通道飞机	上海—悉尼 SHA-SYD	上海虹桥国际机场		8700km	10小时15分钟	中国、菲律宾（Philippines）印度尼西亚（Indonesia）澳大利亚（Australia）	杭州—福州—厦门—汕头—南海—中沙群岛—南沙群岛—三宝颜（Zamboanga）—达尔文（Darwin）—悉尼（Sydney）
		悉尼金斯福德·史密斯国际机场	夏令时自10月31日起，与我国相差3小时；冬令时自3月25日起，与我国相差2小时		10小时45分钟		

飞国际远程航线时，目的地机场所在地常常和我国有很大的时差，且存在冬令时和夏令时的区别，所以在落地广播时，乘务员一定要准确计算当地时间。如实在分不清楚，可请带班乘务长向机长询问，机长在落地前可根据飞行仪表或与当地塔台确认正确时间，这样可以保证广播的准确性。

知识拓展：飞行航线的第一

1. 中华人民共和国第一条航线

1950年8月1日上午8时30分，民航139号飞机自天津起飞，中午经停汉口，下午6时10分安全抵达重庆，这标志着新中国民航最早的国内航线正式开通，我国民航历史进入新的阶段，史称"八一"开航。

2. 世界上第一条国际航线

1919年2月8日，第一条国际航线诞生了（见图2-1）。这条航线是从法国的巴黎，穿越英吉利海峡到英国的伦敦。由于第一条国际航线开辟成功，飞机便逐渐成为人们在国与国之间、大陆与大陆之间来往的重要交通工具。

图 2-1

任务实践

（1）认真阅读"表2-12 上海—新加坡—上海"航线地标，并说出每一项分别代表什么内容。

（2）根据本任务所学内容，选取上述航线地标，练习播报下段广播。

国际远程航班预报到达时间广播词（节选）

女士们，先生们：

本架飞机预计在北京时间_____、当地时间_____到达_____机场。

谢谢！

Ladies and gentlemen,

We will be landing at _____ airport at _____ (a.m./p.m.) Beijing time or _____ (a.m./p.m.) local time.

Thank you.

任务三　华氏与摄氏温度换算表及换算法

任务导入

华氏温标与摄氏温标是两大国际主流的计量温度的标准，华氏温标的单位符号用"℉"表示，摄氏温标的单位符号用"℃"表示。在实际客舱广播时，尤其在航班落地前播报到达时的温度广播中常常会用到温度的换算。

任务要求

通过对本任务的学习，学习者应能熟练地进行华氏、摄氏温标的换算，至少记住20℃、22℃、25℃三个温度的华氏温度，并在广播中灵活运用。

一、两种温标的由来

（一）华氏温标

华氏温标（Fahrenheit temperature scale，符号为 F，单位为℉）由德国物理学家丹尼尔·家百列·华伦海特（Daniel Gabriel Fahrenheit）制定。

华氏温标的规定是：在标准大气压下，冰的熔点为32华氏度，水的沸点为212华氏度。将冰与盐混合后所能达到的最低温度定为0℉，而将人体的正常体温定为100℉，两者之间等分成100个刻度。

（二）摄氏温标

摄氏温标（Celsius scale，符号为 C，单位为℃）由瑞典天文学家安德斯·摄西阿斯（Anders Celsius）制定。摄氏温标的规定是：在标准大气压下，冰的熔点为0摄氏度，水的沸点为100摄氏度，中间划分100等分，每等分为1℃。

二、两种温标的计算方法

（一）摄氏和华氏温标计算公式

摄氏温标计算公式为

$$C = (F - 32) \times \frac{5}{9}$$

式中：C——摄氏温标，℃；

　　　F——华氏温标，℉。

华氏温标计算公式为

$$F = \left(C \times \frac{9}{5} \right) + 32$$

下面通过两个例子介绍华氏和摄氏温度的相互换算方法。

【例1】 68华氏度是多少摄氏度？

运用摄氏温标计算公式，计算出 C 的值：

$$C = (68 - 32) \times \frac{5}{9}$$

$$= 36 \times \frac{5}{9}$$

$$= 20$$

即 20℃ = 68℉。

【例2】 在什么温度下两个温标单位的值一样？

设两个温标单位的值一样时的温度为 T（此时 $C = F = T$），代入华氏温标计算公式，计算出 T：

$$T = T \times \frac{9}{5} + 32$$

$$-32 + T = T \times \frac{9}{5}$$

$$-32 = T \times \frac{4}{5}$$

$$-40 = T$$

即当 $T = -40$ 时，两个温标单位的值相同，也就是 -40℃ = -40℉。

（二）摄氏温标换算为华氏温标心算公式

（1）以20℃和68℉的转换为例：

$$F = C \times 2 - 2\text{倍后的十位数字} + 32$$

$$68℉ = 20℃ × 2 - 2\text{倍后的十位数字} + 32$$
$$68℉ = (20 × 2 - 2\text{倍后的十位数字} + 32)℉$$
$$68℉ = (40 - 4 + 32)℉$$
$$68℉ = (36 + 32)℉$$

（2）以 25℃ 的心算为例：

$$F = C × 2 - 2\text{倍后的十位数字} + 32$$
$$= (25 × 2 - 2\text{倍后的十位数字} + 32)℉$$
$$= (50 - 5 + 32)℉$$
$$= (45 + 32)℉$$
$$= 77℉$$

（注：此公式计算出的华氏温度都是取整数的近似值，在实际广播时，落地前驾驶舱一给出时间和温度，乘务员就要立刻广播了，所以记住这个心算公式在工作中会很有帮助；或者也可以查阅广播词后的摄氏华氏温度表，但是并不是每一个温度都能查阅到的。）

三、华氏和摄氏温度换算简表

华氏和摄氏温度换算简表见表 2-14。

表 2-14 华氏和摄氏温度换算简表

华氏度 /℉	摄氏度 /℃	华氏度 /℉	摄氏度 /℃	华氏度 /℉	摄氏度 /℃	华氏度 /℉	摄氏度 /℃
-47.2	-44	-18.4	-28	10.4	-12	39.2	4
-45.4	-43	-16.6	-27	12.2	-11	41	5
-43.6	-42	-14.8	-26	14	-10	42.8	6
-41.8	-41	-13	-25	15.8	-9	44.6	7
-40	-40	-11.2	-24	17.6	-8	46.4	8
-38.2	-39	-9.4	-23	19.4	-7	48.2	9
-36.4	-38	-7.6	-22	21.2	-6	50	10
-34.6	-37	-5.8	-21	23	-5	51.8	11
-32.8	-36	-4	-20	24.8	-4	53.6	12
-31	-35	-2.2	-19	26.6	-3	55.4	13
-29.2	-34	-0.4	-18	28.4	-2	57.2	14
-27.4	-33	1.4	-17	30.2	-1	59	15
-25.6	-32	3.2	-16	32	0	60.8	16
-23.8	-31	5	-15	33.8	1	62.6	17
-22	-30	6.8	-14	35.6	2	64.4	18
-20.2	-29	8.6	-13	37.4	3	66.2	19

续表

华氏度 /℉	摄氏度 /℃	华氏度 /℉	摄氏度 /℃	华氏度 /℉	摄氏度 /℃	华氏度 /℉	摄氏度 /℃
68	20	78.8	26	89.6	32	100.4	38
69.8	21	80.6	27	91.4	33	102.2	39
71.6	22	82.4	28	93.2	34	104	40
73.4	23	84.2	29	95	35	105.8	41
75.2	24	86	30	96.8	36	107.6	42
77	25	87.8	31	98.6	37	109.4	43

知识拓展：人体温度

人体正常体温（body temperature）测量出的结果取决于在一天中的时间中身体内发生的变化。通常，正常人的体温在早上会较低，在晚上则大约高 0.5℃（0.9℉）。而正常体温一般值：舌下为 36.8±0.4℃（98.2±0.72℉）；体内为 37.0℃（98.6℉）。

身体的不同部位有不同的温度，例如直接测量体腔内部的直肠或阴道的结果通常比口腔的温度稍高，而且口腔的温度比皮肤的温度稍高。其他地方，如在手臂或耳后的正常温度也不相同。

任务实践

（1）默写摄氏温标转华氏温标心算公式，并选取简表的温度进行运算。

（2）根据本任务所学内容，选取华氏（摄氏）温度，练习播报下段广播。

➡ 国内航班落地广播词（节选）⬅

女士们，先生们：

我们已经到达＿＿＿＿机场。现在是北京时间＿＿＿＿点＿＿＿＿分，外面温度＿＿＿＿摄氏度，＿＿＿＿华氏度。

谢谢！

Ladies and gentlemen,

We have just landed at ＿＿＿＿ airport. The local time is ＿＿＿＿. The ground temperature is ＿＿＿＿ degrees centigrade/Celsius or ＿＿＿＿ degrees Fahrenheit.

Thank you.

任务四　各国入境海关检疫规定简述

任务导入

在飞国际远程航线的时候，乘务员常常会在入境前给乘客发放海关、检疫申报表并指导填写，也会有相应的广播。根据国际民航局规定，有些国家如美国、法国等要求国际航班在入境前对机舱喷洒消毒药水，也会有喷洒药水广播。这两类广播都需要乘务员有相关的海关检疫知识。本任务简单列举中国、美国、日本、澳大利亚等国家的相关规定，其中最为严格的则是澳大利亚。

任务要求

通过本任务的学习，学习者应基本了解本任务所列国家海关检疫相关规定，并能自学其他国家的相关规定。

一、中国海关出入境规定

经中华人民共和国海关总署批准实施双通道制的海关监管场所，海关设置申报通道（又称"红色通道"）和无申报通道（又称"绿色通道"）供进出境乘客依本规定选择。

（一）乘客出入境规定

（1）下列进境乘客应向海关申报，并将申报单证交由海关办理物品进境手续：

① 携带需经海关征税或限量免税的《乘客进出境行李物品分类表》第二、三、四类物品（不含免税、限量内的烟酒）者；

② 非居民乘客及持有前往国家（地区）再入境签证的居民乘客携带途中必需的旅行自用物品超出照相机、便携式收录音机、小型摄影机、手提式摄录机、手提式文字处理机每种一件范围者；

③ 携带人民币现钞 6000 元以上，或金银及其制品 50 克以上者；

④ 非居民乘客携带外币现钞折合 5000 美元以上者；

⑤ 居民乘客携带外币现钞折合 1000 美元以上者；

⑥ 携带货物、货样以及携带物品超出乘客个人自用行李物品范围者；

⑦ 携带中国检疫法规规定管制的动、植物及其产品以及其他须办理验放手续的物品者。

（2）下列出境乘客应向海关申报，并将申报单证交由海关办理物品出境手续：

① 携带需复带进境的照相机、便携式收录音机、小型摄影机、手提式摄录机、手提式文字处理机等旅行自用物品者；

② 未将应复带出境物品原物带出或携带进境的暂时免税物品未办结海关手续者；

③ 携带外币、金银及其制品未取得有关出境许可证明或超出本次进境申报数额者；

④ 携带人民币现钞 6000 元以上者；

⑤ 携带文物者；

⑥ 携带货物、货样者；

⑦ 携带出境物品超出海关规定的限值、限量或其他限制规定范围的；

⑧ 携带中国检疫法规规定管制的动、植物及其产品以及其他须办理验放手续的物品者。

（二）乘客携带液态物品规定

乘坐从中国境内机场始发的国际、地区航班的乘客，其随身携带的液态物品每件容积不得超过 100 毫升（mL）。盛放液态物品的容器，应置于最大容积不超过 1 升（L）的、可重新封口的透明塑料袋中。每名乘客每次仅允许携带一个透明塑料袋，超出部分应交运。

（1）液态物品包括：

① 饮品，例如矿泉水、饮料、汤及糖浆；

② 乳霜、护肤液、护肤油、香水及化妆品；

③ 喷雾及压缩容器，例如剃须泡沫及香体喷雾；

④ 膏状物品，例如牙膏；

⑤ 隐形眼镜药水；

⑥ 凝胶，例如头发定型及沐浴用的凝胶产品；

⑦ 任何稠度相似的溶液及物品。

（2）以下物品可以随身携带（超过 100 毫升，必须接受 X 光检查）：

① 药物，只限旅程所需要数量，如糖尿病药物包等乘客必需的液态药品（需凭医生处方或医院证明）；

② 婴儿食品，只限旅程所需要数量，如婴儿奶粉/牛奶/母乳（需有婴儿随行）；

③ 非液态化妆品，如固体止汗剂、唇膏、粉末状粉底。

二、美国海关入境与申报注意事项

目前美国已取消 I-94 出入境表格的填写，因此只需填写海关申报单。填表的时候必须用大写字母填写。海关申报单以每个家庭为单位，必须是直系亲属（如父子、母子、夫妻、亲生兄弟姐妹等）才能够共同填写一张表格，旁系亲属及朋友关系都必须分开单独填写。

（一）海关申报抽查

入境乘客将自己的海关申报单交给海关人员，如果无申报物品则走绿色通道；有申报物品则走红色通道。

1. 告知工作人员未携带任何需要申报的物品

大部分会被安排走绿色通道直接过 X 光，小部分会被抽查走红色通道开箱检查，如果被检查出来后果会比较严重，因为最开始未诚实回答。

2. 告知工作人员有携带一些需申报物品

工作人员会问询大概是什么物品，如实回答即可。大部分情况会安排走红色通道开箱检查，因此收拾行礼时请将不确定的需申报物品放在一起。

对于任何不确定的食品或物品最好都进行申报，也就是在申报单上对于不确定的项目一栏勾选"是"即可。海关人员会进行检查评估，不能入境的会予以没收，不会产生额外的罚款。当然未申报而被查到的将另行处理；对入境的非美国居民来说，除个人自用物品外，如果入境将超过 72 小时，可免税带入 100 美元的商品或礼品，且该免税待遇 6 个月内只可使用 1 次。除个人物品外，任何在美国境外取得的价值超过个人免税额度（100 美元）的物品均需申报。

（二）可免税物品

可免税物品如下。

（1）个人物品，如用于商业目的则需征税。

（2）酒精饮料，21 周岁以上入境者可携带 1L 以下的酒精饮料。

（3）烟草产品，21 周岁以上入境者可携带 200 支香烟或 100 支雪茄。

（4）家庭物品，衣服、珠宝、摄影设备、便携式收音机和车辆应作为个人物品。

（5）免税礼品，为方便检查，不要将礼品进行包装。

（6）邮寄的礼品。

（7）在免税店购买的物品。

（三）禁止和限制入境物品

禁止和限制入境物品如下。

（1）食品，如肉类、鸡蛋。

（2）水果、蔬菜、植物、植物种子及土壤。

（3）违法药物以及包括以下成分中药和中成药。

① 麻黄碱类药物，复方川贝止咳糖浆、感冒胶囊、急支糖浆等；

② 士的宁类，跌打万花油、风湿关节炎片、关节炎膏等；

③ 吗啡类、咳速停、克咳、小儿止泻灵等；

④ 有动物或动物器官，如蝎子、蜈蚣、鹿茸、麝香、燕窝、阿胶等成分的中药或中成药。

（4）钱币和黄金制品，金额低于1万美元。

（5）违反知识产权和注册商标的物品。

（6）鱼、野生动物、宠物。

（7）生物制品。

（8）纺织品和服装。

（9）文化遗产和文物古董。

（10）违禁药物器具。

（11）枪支。

三、英国入境和海关检查注意事项

（一）入境检查

入境处标有"Arrivals"的标识牌会指引乘客到入境大厅（UK Border）；入境检查处的电子显示屏会显示应该通过哪个通道；入境官员会检查乘客文件是否齐全以及是否持有签证和有效护照；检查无误后，入境官员会在护照上盖章标明入境日期。注意入境大厅禁止拍照。

（二）海关检查

通过入境检查后，乘客就可以去领取行李了。乘客可根据电子显示屏上的航班号码，在相应的传送带上找到自己的行李（这些程序和国内的航班一样）。如果发现行李有缺失，应立即与航空公司在机场的办事处联系。

1. 海关申报/无申报通道

领取行李后，下一步是通过海关检查。乘客会看到有以下三个出口。

（1）蓝色通道（blue channel）：如果乘客从欧盟国家出发，走该通道。

（2）绿色通道（green channel）：如果乘客从非欧盟的国家和地区出发，并且没有要申报的物品则走该通道。

（3）红色通道（red channel）：有要申报的物品走这里。

2. 英国海关对烟 / 酒等物品的数量限制

（1）烟草类，每位乘客只能携带 200 支香烟，或者 100 支小雪茄或者 50 支雪茄或者 250g 烟叶。如果超出限量，必须申报，并且补交税款，否则会被没收。

（2）酒类，每人只能携带 4L 的静葡萄酒（still wine），不能是起泡酒，16L 的啤酒，或者 1L 的烈酒（酒精含量超过 22%Vol），2L 的强化葡萄酒（fortified wine），起泡酒或者其他酒精含量低于 22%Vol 的酒精饮品，如果超量限量，必须申报，并且补交税款，否则会被没收。

（3）价值低于 390 英镑的看起来像商品的物品。

（4）药品（仅限个人使用）。

3. 英国海关禁止携带的物品

（1）肉类，牛奶或者其他动物产品。

（2）非法药物（中药类可能会有问题）。

（3）武器（包括某些有攻击型刀具，胡椒喷雾等自卫型武器）。

（4）淫秽物品。

（5）假冒或者盗版商品。

（6）珊瑚、亚马孙森林的木材、象牙、海龟壳等与濒危物种相关物品、宠物以及某些植物的种子和根等。

（7）用受保护动物皮毛做成的衣服及鞋等。

（8）禁止携带无线电传输装置。

4. 其他

2019 年 5 月 20 日开始不再填写英国入境卡。

四、澳大利亚入境海关检疫规定

（一）对烟草的规定

澳大利亚对于携带烟草入境的规定一直在更改，最初可以携带 50 支香烟入境，后来为了严控烟草，限制数量下降为 25 支。目前对于这一项规定的更改，海关表示，这是为了严控烟草走私行为。自 2019 年 7 月 1 日起，任何烟草类商品都禁止携带，如果携带应直接申报，海关将延用之前的烟草税标准。任何烟草类商品都必须申报，按规定补税。

（二）必须申报的物品

入境澳大利亚必须申报的物品见图 2-2 澳大利亚入境乘客登记卡。

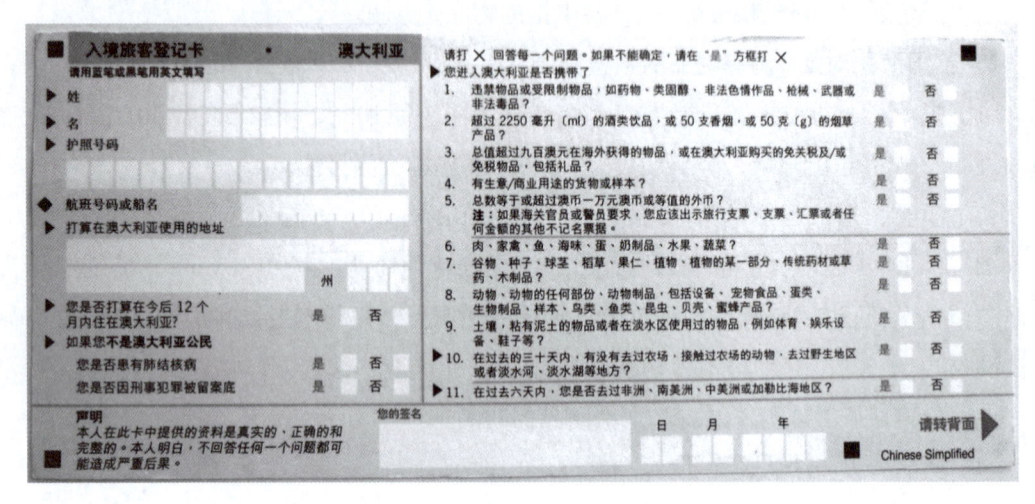

图　2-2

1. 食物

（1）腊肠／肉肠。

（2）盐腌的整只鸭子、鸭肝、鸭肾、鸭肠、牛肉条、牛肉粒、牛肉干、牛肉以及猪肉丝，含猪肉的月饼，含有肉的方便面，猪蹄，烤猪肉，宠物粮食（包括鱼粮及鸟食）。

（3）煮熟及未经烹调的食物及食物材料。

（4）制干、盐腌及新鲜鱼类及海鲜，包括元贝、鱼翅、鱿鱼及鱼肚／花胶。

（5）制干的水果及蔬菜，包括猴头菇、龙眼干、荔枝干、陈皮、话梅、干人参。

（6）面条和米饭。

（7）包装膳食，包括飞机上的食物、汤包香草及香料（八角茴香、肉桂、丁香）。

（8）草药及传统药物、补药及香草茶，如包括陈皮、菊花、树皮、灵芝、党参等。

（9）零食，包括银杏、落花生、瓜子、肉松等。

（10）饼干、糕点及糖果（有猪肉的杏仁饼、威化饼、有猪肉的鸡仔饼、有香肠的糕饼是被禁的）。

（11）茶、咖啡和其他用牛奶冲调的饮品，包括三合一咖啡、茶和美禄等。

（12）茶和柑橘类香料。

2. 动物产品

（1）羽毛、骨、角制品及獠牙（必须是清洁和没有带有任何动物组织）。

（2）皮革、兽皮及皮毛（兽皮制品包括鼓、盾都是被禁的，除非经过处理）。

（3）羊毛或动物毛，包括毛被、毛线和工艺制品等。

（4）动物及雀鸟标本（有些标本可能按照濒危野生动物保护法例而被禁）。

（5）贝壳包括珠宝及纪念品（按照濒危物种保护法例珊瑚是被禁的）。

（6）蜜蜂产品包括蜜糖、蜂巢、蜂王浆及蜂蜡。花粉是被禁的。

（7）使用过的动物装备，包括兽医用的仪器及药物，剪羊毛或肉类商业的工具，鞍具、马具及动物或鸟笼。

（8）宠物粮食及玩物，包括狗的皮制嚼物及鱼粮都是被禁的。

3．植物材料

（1）木制的手工艺品、对象及雕刻，包括着色及漆涂物品（树皮是被禁的，会被取去或需要进行处理）。

（2）用植物材料制造的人工制品、手工艺品及古董。

（3）用植物材料、棕榈叶或树叶制成的席子、袋或其他物品（用芭蕉叶制成的物品是被禁的）。

（4）草制产品包括帽子、席子及包装。

（5）百花香及椰子壳。

（6）含有或填满种子的物品。

（7）干花及干花装饰。

（8）新鲜花卉（可以由茎繁殖的鲜花如玫瑰、康乃馨和菊花都是被禁的）。

4．其他物品

（1）用动物或植物材料制成的手工艺品及嗜好产品。

（2）使用过的运动及露营设备，包括帐篷、自行车、高尔夫球及钓鱼设备，染上泥土、粪便或植物材料的鞋子/远足靴子。

（三）严禁携带入境的物品

以下物品是被禁止及会被没收和销毁的，或乘客可以将物品弃置在机场的检疫箱内。

1．乳制品，蛋及含蛋的产品

（1）所有整个、干的以及粉末的蛋以及含蛋的产品，包括含蛋的面条、含有蛋的月饼（咸蛋、加工过的蛋及皮蛋），盐腌或加工的鸭蛋及鹌鹑蛋，含蛋的方便面及蛋黄酱。

（2）所有乳制品（除非来自一个被列为没有口蹄疫的国家的产品）。成分含有超过10%的乳制品的未加工及干的产品，包括三合一咖啡、茶及美禄、奶粉及有牛奶成分的即食谷物食品。

注意：随同婴儿的婴儿配方及新西兰的乳制品是许可的。

2. 非罐装的肉类产品

所有动物种类的新鲜、制干、冷藏、煮熟、烟熏、盐腌、加工或包装的产品。

3. 活的动物

所有哺乳动物、雀鸟、鸟蛋以及雀巢、鱼、爬虫动物（甲鱼）、蛇、蝎子、两栖动物、甲壳类动物及昆虫。

4. 活的植物

（1）所有盆栽/露出根部的植物、竹、盆景、剪枝、根、球根、球茎、根茎、茎部及其他可以繁殖的植物材料及泥土。

（2）煮熟、制干、新鲜或冷冻的芭蕉叶也是不被允许的。

5. 草药及传统药物

（1）鹿角、鹿茸、鹿角精华、鹿鞭、阿胶，但来自新西兰及标明是新西兰产品的鹿制品是被许可的。

（2）燕窝、冬虫夏草、灵芝。

（3）雪蛤膏、地龙、任何种类的干制动物尸体、紫河车、蛤蚧干、鹿筋、甲鱼、牛尾。

6. 种子及果仁

谷物食品、爆谷、未加工的果仁、生栗子、新鲜花生、松果、鸟食、水果以及蔬菜种子、未经证实种类的种子、一些商业包装的种子、种子及豆制装饰品、山楂、红豆及绿豆。

7. 新鲜水果及蔬菜

所有新鲜以及冷冻的水果和蔬菜，包括蒜头、姜、辣椒、苹果、柿子、柑、草药、新鲜竹笋。

（四）超过免税优惠额度的物品

澳大利亚的免税优惠不同于其他国家，特别需要注意。

（1）年满18岁，可以携带价值最高达900澳元的普通物品入境，并享受免税优惠。未满18岁的限额是450澳元。普通物品包括礼品、纪念品、照相机、电子设备、皮革制品、香精、珠宝、手表和运动器械。

（2）酒类：年满18岁，可以携带2.25L的酒类入境。

（3）家庭成员一同出游可以累加各自的免税优惠。

（4）如果乘客所携带的物品超过了澳大利亚的免税优惠限额，乘客将面临的不仅是为超限的单个物品缴税，而是为携带的所有该类物品缴税。

五、法国入境海关检疫规定

（一）入境法国可携带的免缴海关关税物品

（1）200支香烟或50支雪茄烟、1L烈酒、2L葡萄酒、250mL化妆品、50g香水、500g咖啡、100g茶、自用物品及自用药物。

（2）携带价值1万欧元以上的现金、超过免税限量的自用品、用于商业目的物品入境，须向海关申报。管制药品、动植物、肉制品等限制物品须向海关申报并办理严格的入境手续。

（二）违禁品

毒品、麻醉品、假冒盗版产品、军火、弹药、爆炸物、象牙制品、淫秽物品等均属于违禁品。乘客在机场提取行李后，海关进行例行抽查，如超出限制范围应主动向海关申报，否则将受到海关的处罚。

六、日本海关对入境所携带物品的规定

在飞机廊桥口，检疫所会发给每位乘客身体健康状况表，乘客填写之后，交至检疫所服务窗口。如果在旅行中，乘客有任何发烧、腹痛等不适，都可向"健康相谈室"要求帮助。

日本禁止携带入境品如下。

（1）名牌等仿冒品。

（2）牛、猪、羊等家禽类的肉（包括牛肉干）、内脏及肉食加工品（火腿、热狗、培根、烘干之物等）。

（3）土、附带着土之植物、水果。

（4）象牙、象牙制品及一部分的动物标本、毛皮、皮革制品等，《华盛顿条约》里被指定保护动物的制品、加工品。

（5）其他没有被指定的动植物，必须要在日本检疫柜台接受检疫。部分中药也被指定禁止携带入境。

（6）化妆品及医药品可携带入境，但数量有限制（化妆品一种24个以内）。

七、韩国入境海关规定

（一）海关规定

报关以书面申报为原则（见图2-3韩国入境卡），但乘客所携带的随身行李，口头申

报即可，通过韩国金浦机场的乘客，可自由选择一般有关税或免关税的海关柜台。若乘客所带的物品价值不超韩币 30 万元；行李的重量不超 20 千克；所持外币不超 10000 美元者，皆可在免税的简便柜台办理手续；对于枪炮火药、仿冒品、无线电用品等则不包括在内。

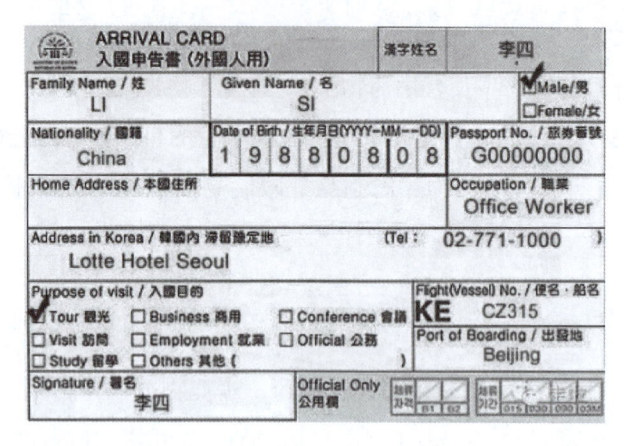

图 2-3

（二）免税物品

入境韩国可免关税物品如下。

（1）随身携带自用衣服、首饰、化妆品及日用品。

（2）香烟 200 支。

（3）酒类一瓶（1000mL）。

（4）香水 2 盎司。

（5）相当于韩币 30 万元以下的礼品。

知识拓展：宠物乘机

中国民航规定，航空公司接受运输的小动物是指家庭驯养的狗、猫、鸟或其他玩赏类宠物，野生动物和具有形体怪异或者易于伤人等特性的动物如蛇等，不能作为行李运输，但可以作为货物运输。

1. 有效证件

检疫证明有效期最长为 7 天，所以乘机日期必须在动物检疫证明的有效期内，一些航空公司还会要求乘客准备好宠物健康证书和航空箱消毒证明。

2. 舱位

航空公司对托运猫狗等宠物有数量限制，乘客要为自己的宠物订到一个有氧舱位，最好提前 3 天以上向航空公司申请。

3．航空箱

航空箱必须符合以下要求。

（1）能防止动物破坏、逃出和伸出容器。

（2）保证空气流通。

（3）能防止粪便渗漏。

4．登机前准备

长途旅行前，宠物需要注射所有疫苗才安全。若旅行时间较长，可咨询兽医，是否需要给宠物服用镇静剂。在寒冷的冬季，可给宠物穿上保暖衣物以免受冻。宠物至少在登机前3小时禁食，并做好排尿工作。乘飞机时，宠物易感口渴，乘客需要在航空箱里固定好够大的饮水器（还可放上部分食物）。乘机当天，乘客需要提前2小时到达机场办理手续，具体地点请咨询服务人员。

任务实践

（1）简述韩国入境海关规定。

（2）列举法国入境的违禁品有哪些？

（3）结合本任务所学内容方法，熟练朗读下段中英文广播词，了解播报的时间规定。

美国检疫规定广播词

女士们、先生们：

根据美国检疫规定，入境的乘客，不能随身携带新鲜水果、肉类、植物以及鲜花等。如您已带上飞机，请您在落地前处理完或交给客舱乘务员处理，我们将乐意为您服务。

谢谢！

Ladies and gentlemen,

According to the requirements of the United States quarantine (/ˈkwɒrəntiːn/), passengers can not bring in fresh fruit, cut flowers, plants or meats. Those passengers in possession (/pəˈzeʃn/) of such items are required to dispose of them or give them to the flight attendants before arrival.

Thank you!

本项目教学音频

实践篇

项目三 基础广播教学

项目目标

知识目标	掌握乘客登机广播的英语生词和句型； 掌握关门—滑行广播的英语生词和句型； 掌握国际航班空中服务广播的英语生词和句型； 掌握国际航班落地滑行广播的英语生词和句型。
技能目标	流利地进行乘客登机广播及情景对话； 流利地进行关门—滑行广播及情景对话； 流利地进行国际航班空中服务广播及情景对话； 流利地进行国际航班落地滑行广播及情景对话。
职业素养目标	培养学生爱岗敬业的精神； 培养学生机上广播职业素养； 培养学生对旅客的主动服务意识。

任务一 乘客登机广播

任务导入

从本项目开始，进入到广播词和相关乘务英语的实际学习。本项目根据国际远程航线乘客登机实际选取基本并具有代表性的广播词，结合机上情景教学。本任务是乘客登机关机门前一个系列的三段广播。

广播要求

语速适中、咬字清晰；语气亲切、自然大方但又要起到提示提醒的作用。其中第3段"禁止使用电子器具"应比前两段广播语速稍快，因为马上就要和地面人员核对舱单，关闭舱门了，也可以使用机上预录广播。

> **任务要求**
>
> 通过对本任务的学习，学习者应能熟练进行三段广播，牢记机上情景对话并演练。

一、乘客登机广播词

1. 登机广播

女士们、先生们：

　　欢迎您乘坐_____航空班机。上机以后请您对号入座，您的座位号码位于行李架下方。请将手提物品放在行李架上，请不要将行李放在走廊、通道及紧急出口处。

　　找到座位的乘客请您尽快入座，以便后面乘客登机。

　　谢谢！

Boarding

Good morning (afternoon/evening), ladies and gentlemen,

　　Welcome aboard _____ Airlines. Please take your seat according to your seat number. Your seat number is on the rack. Please make sure your hand baggage is stored in the overhead locker. Please keep the aisle and the exits clear of baggage.

　　Please take your assigned seats as quickly as possible and keep the aisle(s) clear for others to be seated.

　　Thank you for your cooperation.

2. 防登错机

女士们、先生们：

　　本架飞机是由_____飞往_____的_____航班，（本次航班与_____航空公司_____航班实施代码共享。）请各位乘客再次确认一下您的机票和登机牌，谢谢您的合作。

Boarding Pass Recheck

Ladies and gentlemen,

　　This is _____ Airlines flight _____ which is code-share with _____（外航代码共享航班号）_____ bound for _____ .Would you please check your passenger ticket and boarding pass once again and make sure of your flight number.

Thank you for your cooperation.

3. 禁止使用电子器具

女士们、先生们：

为防止干扰飞行通信和导航系统，请您在飞行全程中不要使用以下电子设备：移动电话、调频调幅收音机、便携式电视机以及遥控装置等。其他电子设备如笔记本电脑等请在起飞十五分钟后使用，但必须在"系好安全带"灯亮后关闭，以便飞机下降。

谢谢您的合作。

Electronic Devices Restriction

Ladies and gentlemen,

Please note certain electronic devices must not be used on board at any time. These devices include mobile phones, AM/FM radios, televisions and remote control equipment. All other electronic devices including laptops must not be switched on until fifteen minutes after take-off, and must be switched off when the seat belt signs come on for landing.

Your cooperation will be much appreciated.

词汇

rack /ræk/	n. 行李架（主要指有凹槽的那部分，也可用 luggage rack）
aisle /aɪl/	n. 通道，走道；侧廊
hand baggage /ˈbæɡɪdʒ/	手提行李
overhead locker	行李架（也可用 overhead compartment）
bound for	开往……
boarding pass	登机牌
remote control equipment	遥控设备/装置
the seat belt sign	系好安全带标志（灯）

二、乘客登机情景用语

1. 登机迎宾

（1）Good morning, madam. Welcome aboard.

早上好，女士。欢迎登机。

（2）Welcome to _____ (airlines/airways).

　　　欢迎搭乘_____航班。

（3）Good afternoon, sir. May I have your boarding pass, please?

　　　下午好，先生。需要我帮您看下登机牌吗？

（4）31A, it's a window seat. This way, please.

　　　31A，是靠窗的座位。请走这边。

　　　15F, please go that way.

　　　15F，请走那边（过道）。

（注：双通道大飞机迎客时有两个过道。）

2. 引导乘客座位

（1）May I help you, sir?

　　　先生，有什么需要帮忙的吗？

　　　May I lead you to your seat?

　　　需要我带您到您的座位吗？

（2）Your seat is across from that aisle.

　　　您的座位在另一个过道。

　　　Your seat is in next cabin. Please go straight on.

　　　您的座位在下个位舱。请往前走。

　　　Your seat number is 11D. It's an aisle seat. Please come with me.

　　　您的座位是11D，是一个过道座位。请跟我来。

（注：因为是服务人员，所以尽量不用 follow。）

（3）Excuse me, sir. Could you please wait to put in your luggage, so that the passengers behind you can pass through?

　　　不好意思，先生。你能不能等一下再放行李，让后面的乘客先过一下？

（4）Here is your seat. Enjoy the/your flight.

　　　这是您的座位。祝您旅途愉快。

3. 协助乘客摆放行李

（1）Please be careful. Let me help you with your luggage.

　　　请小心。让我来帮您放行李吧。

　　　I'm afraid the overhead locker is full.

　　　不好意思，上方的行李架满了。

　　　May I suggest that you put it under the seat in front of you?

　　　您的包可以放在您前面座椅的下方吗？

（2）I'm afraid that your baggage is too big. We need to put it into the cargo.

不好意思，您的行李太大了，客舱放不下。我们需要把它放入货舱。

Please take it and come with me. Our ground staff there will handle it.

请带上行李跟我走。我们的地面人员正等在机门边，她会帮您办理相关手续。

（注：大件行李必须请乘客配合托运，否则会影响客舱安全。）

Later after landing you can claim it at the baggage claim area.

到站后，请到行李转盘处提取您的行李。

（注：在飞机上托运行李后，地面人员会将托运行李牌交给乘务员再转交给乘客，这时候需要向乘客解释下机提取行李发地方。通常要比正常托运的行李晚到行李转盘或者跟随下一班飞机到达。）

词汇

go straight on	直走
an aisle seat	（一个）过道座位
cargo /ˈkɑːgəʊ/	n. 货物，货舱
handle /ˈhændl/	v. 处理；对付（某人或某事）
baggage claim area	行李提取处 / 行李转盘

句型

（1）Please keep the aisle and the exits clear of baggage.

请保持过道和出口处畅通（请不要在过道和出口处放置行李）。

（2）Please take your assigned seats as quickly as possible.

请尽快按号入座。

（3）Thank you for your cooperation.

感谢您的配合。

（4）Certain electronic devices must not be used on board at any time.

在飞机上，有些电子产品任何时候都不能使用。

（5）I'm afraid that the overhead locker is full.

不好意思（我恐怕 / 发现 / 觉得）行李架已经满了。

知识拓展：乘客登机行李处置案例

某航班上，乘务员引导乘客入座时，见一乘客站在座位上往行李架内推箱子，箱子看上去非常重。乘务员正要上前帮忙，箱子突然掉下，乘务员本能地用手去挡箱子，箱子先砸到乘务员的左手，又砸到椅背上，碰到后一排乘客的右前额，乘客被砸处立刻肿了起来。乘务员立即用冰块为其冷敷，并报告机长呼叫急救中心及通知地面有关人员。在医生的建议下，受伤乘客取消了航班，待进一步检查，该箱子的主人也一同下了飞机（见图3-1）。

图 3-1

案例分析

（1）乘客登机时，乘务员发现乘客超大、超重行李应通知地面办理托运手续。

（2）客舱内迎客的乘务员应仔细观察上机乘客的状况，及时主动地帮助需要帮助的乘客，避免上述情况的发生。

任务实践

（1）熟读三段广播词，进行客舱广播实练。

（2）在所给词汇后填写对应的中文或英文。

行李提取处＿＿＿＿＿＿＿＿＿＿　　overhead locker ＿＿＿＿＿＿＿＿＿

遥控设备/装置＿＿＿＿＿＿＿＿＿　　clear of ＿＿＿＿＿＿＿＿＿

手提行李＿＿＿＿＿＿＿＿＿＿　　switch on ＿＿＿＿＿＿＿＿＿

航班号＿＿＿＿＿＿＿＿＿＿＿　　switch off ＿＿＿＿＿＿＿＿＿

尽快地＿＿＿＿＿＿＿＿＿＿＿　　window seat ＿＿＿＿＿＿＿＿＿

（3）单项选择题。

① You should take your ＿＿＿＿ seats as quickly as possible.

　A. signed　　　　　　　　　　　B. assigned

　C. ordered　　　　　　　　　　　D. booked

② The lavatory ＿＿＿＿ not be used when taking off or descending.

　A. can　　　　　　　　　　　　　B. may

　C. must　　　　　　　　　　　　　D. will

③ Electronic devices _____ laptop computers must not be switched on.

  A. including   B. included   C. includes   D. include

④ Please put in your luggage soon _____ the passengers behind you can pass.

  A. for   B. so that   C. such that   D. as

⑤ Please remain seated _____ the SEAT-BELT sign is off.

  A. when   B. if   C. until   D. while

（4）句子翻译。

① 请不要将行李放在走廊、通道及紧急出口处。

② 请各位乘客再次确认一下您的机票和登机牌，谢谢您的合作。

③ 为防止干扰飞行通信和导航系统，请您在飞行全程中不要使用手机。

④ 您的座位在下个舱位，请往前走。

⑤ 不好意思，您的行李太大了，客舱放不下。我们需要把它放入货舱。

⑥ Certain electronic devices must not be used on board at any time.

⑦ Electronic devices must be switched off when the seat-belt signs come on for landing.

⑧ Your cooperation will be much appreciated.

⑨ May I suggest that you put it under the seat in front of you?

⑩ Later after landing you can claim it at the baggage claim area.

（5）参考课文中的知识拓展，用英语填空，并分组完成角色演练。

PX: passenger, FA: flight attendant. (Passenger X is carrying a huge suitcase onboard.)

PX: Hi, come on. I need your help.

FA: Sorry, sir, _____. We need to put it into the cargo.

PX: What? I have so many important things in it. I should take it with me.

FA: Sorry, sir. It's too big. We cannot put it into _____, what's more, it's the safety requirement that the suitcase bigger than 20 inches must be consigned. You have a 24 inches one.

PX: Please, please. It's very very crucially important to me.

FA: I can understand you, sir, we all like to keep important things along. But such a big suitcase may cause dangers in flying. May I suggest you take out the relatively important things out into a bag with you?

PA: That sounds good. But what about the suitcase?

FA: Don't worry. _____. Our ground staff there will handle it.

PA: Well, how can I take it back after landing?

FA: _____.

任务二　关门—滑行广播

任务导入

关闭舱门后，要进行客舱安全设备录像的播放，如果录像故障或者旧机型无录像设备，那么乘务组将进行客舱安全设备示范。（此篇广播词将在后面应急广播词中介绍）接着正常情况下，飞机开始滑行，朗读欢迎词广播，直到起飞前，进行再次确认安全带广播。

广播要求

咬字清晰、语气亲切。第二段确认安全带广播语速稍偏快，有提醒的作用，同时广播的乘务员自己要坐好，系好乘务员座椅安全带，此段广播建议背诵，因为广播词手册属于松散物品，起飞或降落时不宜携带。

任务要求

通过本任务学习，学习者应能熟练进行两段广播，牢记机上情景对话并演练。

一、关门—滑行广播词

➡ 1. 欢迎词 ⬅

尊敬的各位乘客及_____（航空联盟或航空俱乐部）会员们：

早上好（下午好/晚上好）！

我谨代表本次航班的机长_____先生、客舱经理（乘务长）_____女士/先生及全体机组人员欢迎您乘坐_____航空班机，也很高兴地欢迎_____会员再次乘坐_____航空班机。

（今天由于航路天气/航路交通管制/机场跑道繁忙原因，延误了航班起飞，对于您的理解我们深表感谢。）（提示：以上为非航空公司原因）

（今天由于飞机晚到/等待乘客装货/飞机排除故障的原因，延误了本次航班的起飞，耽误了您的行程，为此我们深表歉意。）（提示：以上为航空公司原因）

本次航班前往_____（中途降落_____），（本次航班与_____航班实施代码共享，）由_____到_____的飞行时间预计_____，我们希望与您一起度过这段温馨而愉快的旅程。

飞机马上就要起飞了，请您系紧安全带，收起小桌板，调直椅背，打开遮光板，并请您在飞行全程中关闭手机或将手机调至飞行模式，禁止吸烟。

祝您旅途愉快！

谢谢！

➡ Welcome Address ⬅

Ladies and gentlemen,

Good morning (afternoon/evening)!

On behalf of Captain Mr._____, the cabin manager (purser) Mr/Ms_____, I extend a warm welcome to you aboard _____ Airlines. To members of _____ (club), we are happy to see you again!

(The flight was delayed due to unfavorable weather conditions enroute/air traffic control/airport congestion. Thank you for your patience and understanding.)

(The flight was delayed due to late arrival of the aircraft/waiting for some passengers/cargo loading/mechanical reason. Once again, we do sincerely apologize for the delay of our flight. Thank you for your patience and understanding.)

Our flying time to _____ (destination) is about _____ hour(s) and _____ minute(s). (Our flight is code-share with _____.) We are looking forward to making this flight an enjoyable and comfortable experience for all of you.

Ladies and gentlemen, we will be taking off in a few minutes, please fasten your seat-belt, place your seat back upright, secure your (tray) table, open the window shade, and during the whole flight please keep your mobile phone off or in flight mode and refrain from smoking.

Wish you a pleasant journey.

Thank you!

2.（起飞前）再次确认安全带

女士们、先生们：

飞机马上就要起飞了，请您再次确认安全带已扣好、系紧，所有电子设备已关闭。

谢谢！

Seat-belt Recheck

Ladies and gentlemen,

Our aircraft is going to take off, please make sure that your seat-belt is securely fastened, and all the electronic devices have been switched off.

Thank you!

词汇

unfavorable /ʌnˈfeɪvərəbl/	adj. 不利的，有害的，不赞成的
enroute	adv. 在途中
congestion /kənˈdʒestʃən/	n. 拥挤；拥塞
mechanical /məˈkænɪkl/	adj. 机械的
seat back	座椅靠背
refrain from doing sth	（暂时）克制不做某事
recheck /riːˈtʃek/	vt. 再次核对，再次检查

二、关门—滑行情景用语

1. 起飞前

（1）We are going to take off.

我们很快就要起飞。

（2）For your safety, please fasten the seat-belt.

为了您的安全，请系好安全带。

Please put your seat back upright, stow your table and footrest.

请调直座椅靠背，收起小桌板和脚踏板。

（3）Please put it in the overhead locker.

请放入上方行李架中。

Please put it under the seat.

请放在座位下面。

May I stow your bag into the overhead locker?

我可以帮您把包放在行李架里吗？

（4）May I ask you to pull up the sunshade?

能请您打开遮光板吗？

2. 禁用电子设备

（1）Would you please switch off your mobile phone?

您可以关闭手机吗？

（2）We ask all our passengers to keep the electronic devices off for take-off and landing.

我们要求所有的乘客在起飞和降落时关闭电子设备。

（3）It may interfere with the aircraft navigation system. It has't been allowed to use on board by Civil Aviation Administration of China.

它会干扰飞机导航系统。它没有得到中国民用航空局的认可。

词汇

stow /stəʊ/	vt. 装载；收藏；使暂留
sunshade /ˈsʌnʃeɪd/	n. 遮阳伞；天棚；遮光板（也可用 window shade）
navigation /ˌnævɪˈgeɪʃn/	n. 航行；航海
interfere /ˌɪntəˈfɪə(r)/	vi. 干扰，干涉；妨碍
Civil Aviation Administration of China	中国民用航空局（缩写为 CAAC）

句型

（1）On behalf of _____, I extend a warm welcome to you aboard.

我谨代表_____，欢迎您登机。

（2）The flight was delayed due to bad weather enroute.

因天气原因，本次航班未能按时起飞。

（3）We do sincerely apologize for the delay of our flight.

我们就航班延误表示诚挚的歉意。

（4）Please keep your mobile phone off or in flight mode.

请将您的手机保持关机（状态）或飞行模式。

（5）Please make sure that your seat-belt is securely fastened.

请确认/确保您的安全带已经系好。

知识拓展：安全检查情景案例

某航班，乘客投诉在安全检查时，一位乘务员不是用礼貌和蔼的语气告知他收直椅背，而是用粗鲁的动作连拍五下椅背，这种恶劣的态度让他无法忍受。

案例分析

乘务员提醒或规劝乘客时，应有礼有节，让乘客心悦诚服，不规范的服务非但无效果，而且常常适得其反（见图3-2）。

图 3-2

任务实践

（1）熟读第 1 段广播词，背诵第 2 段广播词，进行客舱广播实练。

（2）在所给词汇后填写对应的中文或英文。

欢迎词＿＿＿＿＿＿＿＿＿＿　　on behalf of ＿＿＿＿＿＿＿＿＿＿

表示热烈欢迎＿＿＿＿＿＿　　due to ＿＿＿＿＿＿＿＿＿＿＿＿

空中交通管制＿＿＿＿＿＿　　airport congestion ＿＿＿＿＿＿＿

导航系统＿＿＿＿＿＿＿＿　　refrain from smoking ＿＿＿＿＿＿

关机＿＿＿＿＿＿＿＿＿＿　　electronic devices ＿＿＿＿＿＿＿

（3）单项选择题。

① During the flight, please ＿＿＿＿ your mobile phone ＿＿＿＿.

　A. keep; off　　B. switch; off　　C. keep; switch off　　D. switch off; /

② When you adjust your seat, please do not ＿＿＿＿ the passengers around you.

　A. interrupt　　B. disturb　　C. interfere　　D. invade

③ We sincerely apologize ＿＿＿＿ the delay and thank you ＿＿＿＿ your patience and understanding.

　A. for; for　　B. with; at　　C. at; for　　D. with; at

④ Please keep your seatbelt ＿＿＿＿ and your seatback ＿＿＿＿.

　A. fastened; upright　　　　B. upright; fasten

　C. fasten; uprighted　　　　D. uprighted; fastened

⑤ Which of the followings is NOT the organization in Civil Aviation?

　A. ICAO　　B. IATA　　C. CAAC　　D. CATTI

（4）句子翻译。

① 我谨代表本次航班的机长麦克（Mike）先生、客舱经理杰茜（Jessy）女士及全体机组人员欢迎您乘坐西部航空（West Airlines）班机。

＿＿＿＿＿＿＿＿＿＿＿＿＿＿＿＿＿＿＿＿＿＿＿＿＿＿＿＿＿＿＿＿＿＿＿＿

② 对于您的理解和耐心等待，我们深表感谢。

＿＿＿＿＿＿＿＿＿＿＿＿＿＿＿＿＿＿＿＿＿＿＿＿＿＿＿＿＿＿＿＿＿＿＿＿

③ 耽误了您的行程，为此我们深表歉意。

＿＿＿＿＿＿＿＿＿＿＿＿＿＿＿＿＿＿＿＿＿＿＿＿＿＿＿＿＿＿＿＿＿＿＿＿

④ 请您在飞行中全程关闭手机。

＿＿＿＿＿＿＿＿＿＿＿＿＿＿＿＿＿＿＿＿＿＿＿＿＿＿＿＿＿＿＿＿＿＿＿＿

⑤ 请您确认安全带已扣好、系紧。

⑥ The flight was delayed due to unfavorable weather conditions enroute.

⑦ We are looking forward to making this flight an enjoyable and comfortable experience for all of you.

⑧ We will be taking off in a few minutes, please fasten your seat-belt, place your seat back upright, secure your (tray) table, open the window shade.

⑨ We ask all our passengers to keep the electronic devices off for take-off and landing.

⑩ It may interfere with the aircraft navigation system.

（5）参考课文中的知识拓展用英文填空，并分组完成角色演练。

(Passenger A is still making a phone call during take-off.)

FA: Excuse me, sir, may I ask you to _____? The aircraft is _____.

PX: Just a moment, it's an urgent call.

FA: Sorry sir, _____, so please switch off your phone now.

PX: Really? So serious? OK.

FA: Thank you _____, and wish you _____.

任务三　国际航班空中服务广播（一）
——平飞—落地前供餐广播

任务导入

由于国际远程航空空中服务的广播最完备，所以本任务摘选了国际航空的空中服务的广播用于教学。本任务选择三段从国际航班平飞到落地前供餐具有代表性的广播。

广播要求

语速偏慢、咬字清晰；语气亲切、信息准确。第一段广播难度最大，信息很容易混淆，所以乘务员一定要准确无误地播报，语速不能快。第二段广播也偏难，播报的语速也不宜过快，免税品销售一般为第一餐送完后播报，以免打扰乘客休息。此三段广播的时间点都是乘客听广播最认真的时候，需要乘务员具备准确熟练的航程及供餐流程知识。

任务要求

通过本任务的学习，学习者应能够熟练进行三段广播，牢记机上情景对话并演练。

一、平飞—落地前供餐广播词

1. 远程航线起飞后

女士们、先生们：

现在我们已经离开_____前往_____。由_____至_____的飞行距离为_____千米，预计空中飞行时间为_____小时_____分钟。

在整个旅途中，我们为您准备了_____餐（早餐/午餐/晚餐）、小零食和_____饮料。

我们将在_____（一般为30）分钟后为您提供_____餐。旅途中我们还为您准备了三明治快餐，飞机到达_____机场前_____小时（一般为2小时左右）我们将为您提供_____餐。

现在您可以使用笔记本电脑，但在飞机下降或机组特别要求时，请关闭笔记本电脑。（再过一会儿黎明即将来临，我们建议您休息前拉下遮光板。）

在整个航班中如果您需要帮助，请随时告诉我们，我们非常乐意为您服务。有兴趣加入_____（航空联盟/航空俱乐部）的乘客，您可以向客舱乘务员领取入会申请表。

谢谢！

After Take-off (International Long-hauls)

Ladies and gentlemen,

The aircraft has left for _____. The air distance from _____ to _____ is _____ kilometers and the estimated flying time is _____ hour(s) and _____ minute(s).

During this long trip, we will provide you _____ ((a) snack), and (a) _____, along with a choice of beverages.

We would like to start our inflight service _____ minutes later. Sandwiches are available throughout the flight. Approximately, _____ hours before arrival in _____ (destination), we will be serving you _____.

Now, lap-top can be used till the aircraft descends or upon captain demands.

(As sunrise will be with us in a few hours, we suggest that you lower the sunshade before going to sleep.)

If there is anything else we can do to make this journey more comfortable for you, please don't hesitate to call us. We are glad to serve you. For those passengers who wish to join us, application forms are available on this flight.

Thank you!

（注：此段广播词有很多信息点，也是难点，乘务员在广播之前一定要和带班乘务长或客舱经理确认好时间等信息才能播报。"（ ）"中的内容均为解释，不必读出。中文第二段"快餐"及英文的"snack"信息段根据航空是否提供小零食而播报，最后一段内容为邀请乘客入会播报。）

2. 免税品销售

女士们、先生们：

我们现在为您提供机上免税商品销售服务，欢迎各位选购。

各种货品均标有美元价格，如果您想了解其他货币的标价，请向乘务员询问。为了方便您机上购物，我们还接受美元旅行支票和国际信用卡。详细信息请查阅您座椅前口袋里的免税品参考目录（见图3-3）。

谢谢！

图 3-3

Duty-free Sale

Ladies and gentlemen,

We are now pleased to offer you a wide selection of exclusive duty-free items which are available on our flight today.

All items are priced in US dollars, please ask our flight attendants for prices in other currencies. We are also pleased to accept credit cards as well as US traveler's cheque.

For detailed information, please check our duty-free catalog located in the seat pocket in front of you.

Thank you!

（注：乘务员根据每个航班免税品收款的具体要求进行广播。）

3. 落地前供餐

女士们、先生们：

我们将于_____小时_____分钟后降落在_____机场，现在我们将为您供应早餐（正餐）和多种饮料。欢迎您选用。

谢谢！

Meal Service (Before Landing)

Ladies and gentlemen,

We will arrive at _____ airport in about _____ hours and _____ minutes. Now we are going to serve breakfast (dinner) and beverages. You are welcome to take your choice.

Thank you.

词汇

estimated /ˈestɪmət/	adj. 估计的；预计的；估算的
approximately /əˈprɒksɪmətli/	adv. 大约，近似地；近于
hesitate /ˈhezɪteɪt/	vi. 踌躇，犹豫；不愿
	vt. 踌躇，犹豫；有疑虑，不愿意
application form	申请表，申请书
available /əˈveɪləbl/	adj. 可获得的；可购得的；可找到的；有空的
exclusive /ɪkˈskluːsɪv/	adj. 独有的；排外的；专一的
currency /ˈkʌrənsi/	n. 货币
US traveller's cheque	美元旅行支票
detailed /ˈdiːteɪld/	adj. 详细的，详尽的
catalog /ˈkætəlɒg/	n. 目录；一览表
dinner /ˈdɪnə(r)/	n. 晚餐，晚宴；宴会；正餐

二、送餐服务情景用语

1. 提供餐食

（1）We are now serving you dinner.

我们现在为您提供晚餐。

Please enjoy your meal.

请慢用。

（2）We have chicken rice and beef noodle. Which one would you like to have?

我们有鸡肉饭和牛肉面。请问您想要哪种？

Would you like pork rice or seafood noodle?

您要猪肉饭还是海鲜面？

（3）I am sorry. We are out of seafood rice.

对不起，海鲜饭已经没有了。

Would you like to try something else? We have beef noodle.

要不要试试别的？我们有牛肉面。

It's a little spicy.

稍有点辣。

（4）Have you reserved children meal?

请问您预订过儿童餐吗？

Here is the vegetarian meal you ordered.

这是您预订的素食餐。

Have you reserved vegetarian meal?

请问您预订过素食餐吗？

I'm sorry that there's no vegetarian meal left.

不好意思，我们没有多余的素食餐。

But we can offer you salad, fruits and bread roll instead.

但我们可以给您色拉、水果和面包。

2. 提供面包

（1）Would you like some bread?

请问您需要面包吗？

（2）Here is the bread for you. Please enjoy.

这里您的面包，请慢用。

（3）Here is the butter for you.

给您黄油。

3. 清理空杯、餐盘

（1）Would you mind passing me your tray please?

麻烦您把餐盘递给我好吗？

（2）May I take it away, madam?
　　我能收走您的餐盘吗，女士？

（3）May I have your tray, please?
　　我能收走您的餐盘吗？

（4）Could you pass me your tray please?
　　能请您把餐盘递给我吗？

（5）Did you enjoy your lunch, madam?
　　午餐用得好吗，女士？

（6）Sir, may I collect your tray? How about the meal?
　　先生，餐盘可以收了吗？您对今天的餐食还满意吗？

词汇

spicy /ˈspaɪsi/	adj. 辛辣的；香的，多香料的
reserve /rɪˈzɜːv/	v. 预订（餐食、座位等）
vegetarian meal	素食餐
bread roll	面包卷；小餐包
tray /treɪ/	n. 托盘；餐盘
collect /kəˈlekt/	vt. 收集；募捐
	vi. 收集；聚集；募捐

句型及短语

（1）The flight distance from A to B is 2000 kilometers.
　　A 地到 B 地的飞行距离是 2000 千米。

（2）on/upon the captain demands
　　服从机长指挥

（3）During this long haul...
　　在长途飞行期间……

（4）If there is anything else we can do, ...
　　如果有我们可以做的其他事情，……

（5）Please don't hesitate to call us.
　　请您随时告诉我们。

（6）We are pleased /It's our pleasure to offer you...
我们非常荣幸地向您推荐……

（7）Please check our duty-free catalog located in the seat pocket.
请查看（位于）座椅口袋里的免税品目录。

（8）Would you mind passing me your tray, please?
请把餐盘递给我好吗？

知识拓展：餐饮服务

某航班，乘务员按正常服务顺序逐一收餐盘，一位带孩子的乘客提出先将她的餐盘收走，以防孩子乱抓食物。乘务员便立即收走了该女士的餐盘。此时另一位乘客认为："该收我的餐盘了，为何先收别人的？"为此，该乘客抱怨乘务员未按工作程序操作，虽然该乘务员向他作了解释（见图3-4），但乘客却认为是在找借口推卸责任。

案例分析

当乘务员为带孩子的乘客提供特殊服务而暂时未按正常程序工作时，应及时与受影响的乘客做好解释。上述案例中，乘务员应事先和该乘客打声招呼"请稍等片刻"以消除乘客的不被尊重感。收好带孩子乘客的餐盘后，再收该乘客餐盘时，语言应跟上"对不起，让您久等了，我这就收走您的餐盘。"这样，相信乘客能予以理解。

图 3-4

任务实践

（1）重点练习第1段广播词，进行三段广播词客舱实练。

（2）在所给词汇后填写对应的中文或英文。

提供晚餐_____   air distance _____
免税品_____   inflight service _____
美元旅行支票_____ approximately _____
预计飞行时间_____ detailed information _____
信用卡_____   application form _____

（3）单项选择题。

① The aircraft has left _____ Nanning.

   A. to   B. with   C. for   D. at

② For those who want to join in the club, application forms are _____ online.

   A. available   B. unavailable   C. avalanche   D. average

③ Please ask our flight attendant for prices in other _____.

   A. cash   B. money   C. currencies   D. current

④ For _____ information, please check the catalog _____ in the seat pocket in front of you.

   A. detail; locate   B. detailed; locate

   C. detail; located   D. detailed; located

⑤ Now we are going to _____ breakfast/dinner and beverages.

   A. serve   B. serve with   C. service   D. serve for

（4）句子翻译。

① 各种货品均标有美元价格，如果您想了解其他货币的标价，请向乘务员询问。
_____

② 我们有鸡肉饭和牛肉面。请问您想要哪种？
_____

③ 麻烦您把餐盘递给我好吗？
_____

④ 请问您预订过儿童餐吗？
_____

⑤ 我们将于1小时30分钟后降落在成都天府国际机场。
_____

⑥ We are also pleased to accept credit cards as well as US traveler's cheque.
_____

⑦ We suggest that you should put on coats or blankets before going to sleep.
_____

⑧ Electronic devices can be used till the aircraft descends or upon captain demands.
_____

⑨ If there is anything else we can do to make this journey more comfortable for you, please don't hesitate to call us.
_____

⑩ May I collect your tray, sir? And how do you like the meal?

（5）参考课文中的知识拓展用英文填空，并分组完成角色演练。

(The flight attendant is serving lunch.)

FA: Excuse me, sir, we are serving lunch. _____.

PX: Well, I am a vegan, can I have some vegetarian diet?

FA: _____?

PX: Well, I think so. My secretary helped me reserved your airline.

FA: OK, just a moment, we will have a check.(several seconds later)

FA: Excuse me, Mr. Jackson. I've got your reservation, and my colleague is coming to serve your vegetarian meal._____.

PA: Never mind. Thanks.

任务四　国际航班空中服务广播（二）
——落地与中转广播

任务导入

国际远程航空落地前除了到达地的时间天气播报，还有中转信息播报和落地前致谢广播等，本任务就选取了这三段广播帮助大家学习。

广播要求

语速偏慢、咬字清晰；语气亲切、信息准确。第一和第二段广播词比第三节的广播词总体上都要难，既需要反复练习与矫音，也需要乘务员有准确中转航班和目的地气候、时差知识。

任务要求

通过本任务的学习，学习者应能熟练进行三段广播，牢记机上情景对话并演练。

一、落地与中转广播词

1. 预报到达时间和目的地的天气

女士们、先生们：

本架飞机预计在北京时间_____点_____分，_____（始发站/目的地）时间_____点_____分到达机场。_____（目的地）的地面温度_____摄氏度，_____华氏度。（当地时间比北京时间早/晚_____小时，如果您需要调整时间，您可以将您的手表向前/后拨_____小时。）_____（目的地）今日的天气为_____（晴天/多云/阴/小雨等）。

（下段广播词可根据到达站实际情况进行选择性广播）

（1）请您注意温度变化，适时增减衣物。（适用于两地温差较大的航班）

（2）现在适逢雨季，出行时请带好雨具。

（3）现在正值_____（寒冬/酷暑）季节，出行时请注意_____（保暖/防暑）。

谢谢！

Time and Weather

Ladies and gentlemen,

We will soon be landing at _____ airport at _____ (Beijing time)/ _____ (destination time). The ground temperature is _____ degrees centigrade and _____ degrees Fahrenheit. (The local time is _____ hour(s) ahead of/behind Beijing time, so you can reset your watch ahead/back _____ hour(s).)

The weather there is _____ (sunny/cloudy/overcast/rainy etc.).

(Reminder)

(1) Due to the temperature change evidently, please take care when going out.

(2) During this rainy season, may we remind you to take umbrella or raincoat when going out.

(3) In this severe winter/high summer, please take care when going out.

Thank you!

（注：如果始发站/目的地时间与北京时间有时差，预报到达时间时必须播报两地时间。）

2. 洛杉矶/旧金山机场中转

女士们、先生们：

如您乘坐_____班机在洛杉矶/旧金山机场中转到美国国内各地或其他国家，当您办完美国移民局入境和海关手续后，请到出口处，地面工作人员将在那里等您，并引导您前往中转航班候机厅办理转机手续。

中转_____（本次航班号）/_____（共享航班号，如 AA7132）代码共享航班的乘客，请您佩戴好中转乘客标志牌，办完入境和海关手续后，请将托运行李交中转柜台工作人员，然后根据机场航班信息系统中显示的登机口号码或工作人员的指示直接前往联程航班登机，再次登机。另外，持有_____航空联程或来回程机票的乘客，请您务必在航班起飞前72小时，办理座位确认手续。

谢谢！

➡ Transfer at LAX/SFO ⬅

Ladies and gentlemen,

In order to provide our best service for those passengers with connecting flights today, after you are cleared with immigration and Customs formalities, please proceed to the interline desk outside the Customs. Our ground staff will guide you to the terminals.

Code-share _____（本次航班号）/ _____（共享航班号，如 AA7132）passengers, please be sure to put on the identification stickers, after you are cleared with immigration and Customs formalities, present the check-in baggage to the Specific Transfer Desk, then proceed directly to the departure gate according to the gate number in flight information display system or instructions of _____ Airlines representatives. Moreover, those passengers who have reserved seats on a connecting or return flight should reconfirm your reservation no later than 72 hours prior to the departure of the flight.

Thank you!

（注：本段广播在预报到达时间、温度后进行广播。共享航班号和联程航班号一定要确认无误再广播。）

➡ 3. 下降与致谢 ⬅

女士们、先生们：

我们将在_____（一般为30）分钟后到达_____机场。现在飞机已经开始下降，请您系紧安全带，收起小桌板（和脚蹬），调直座椅靠背，打开遮光板，关闭正在使用的电子设备。

尊敬的各位乘客，感谢您选择_____航空，和我们共同渡过了这段愉快的航程，有了您的加入，_____航空才会更加精彩。

我们希望能再次为您服务。

谢谢！

> **Descending**

Ladies and gentlemen,

  We will be arriving at _____ airport in _____ minutes. Please fastened your seat-belt, secure your table (and footrest), place your seat back upright, open the sunshade and switch off all the electronic devices.

  Ladies and gentlemen, thank you for choosing _____ Airlines/Airways. We are glad to serve you again.

  Thank you!

词汇

overcast /ˌəʊvəˈkɑːst/	adj. 阴天的；阴暗的
evidently /ˈevɪdəntli/	adv. 显然，明显地；清楚地
connecting flights	联程航班，转机航班
a return flight	回程航班
flight information display system	航班信息系统
reconfirm one's reservation	再次确认预订（机票、酒店）
prior to	在……之前（的）

二、预报时间和乘客中转情景用语

1. 时间和天气

（1）It's raining in Nanjing.

  南京在下雨。

  The fog is heavy at ground level.

  地面的雾很大。

  Sorry, there is a typhoon in Xiamen. It's blowing hard.

  抱歉，厦门正在刮台风，风很大。

  It's snowing today.

  今天下雪。

（2）The temperature is minus three degrees centigrade.

  气温是 −3℃（零下三摄氏度）。

（3）Tokyo time is 6:00 a.m. now.

现在是东京时间早上 6 点。

It is three past five in the morning in Beijing.

北京时间是 5:03（五点零三分）。

（4）One hour ahead of/behind Shanghai.

比上海早 / 晚一个小时。

There is no time difference/jet lag between south Korea and Japan.

韩国和日本的时间是一样的。

We will be delayed for 20 minutes.

我们将延迟 20 分钟。

2. 中转

Madam, I understand. Don't worry. Let me help you. Please write down the connecting fight number. I will ask our ground staff to check it. Please wait a moment. I will be back soon.

女士，我知道了。别担心，我来帮您解决。请将您的后续航班的号码写下来。我会让我们的地勤人员为您查询。请稍等，我马上回来。

词汇

at ground level	在地面上
blow /bləʊ/	v.（风）吹；喘气；吹气
time difference/jet lag /læg/	时差
ground staff	地勤人员

句型

（1）The local time is 2 hours ahead/behind Beijing time, so you can reset your watch ahead/back 2 hours.

当地时间比北京时间早 / 晚 2 个小时，（所以 / 因此）您可以将手表调前 / 后 2 个小时。

（2）May we remind you to take umbrella or raincoat when going out.

我们提醒您外出要带雨伞或雨衣。

（3）In order to provide our best service for those passengers...

为了将我们最好的服务提供给这些乘客……

（4）Please be sure to put on the identification stickers.

请务必带好身份（中转乘客）识别标签。

（5）Please reconfirm your reservation no later than 72 hours prior to the departure of the flight.

请在航班起飞前至少 72 小时再次确认您的（座位）预订。

知识拓展：安全检查

某航班，乘客投诉：飞机在下降过程中，一些心急的乘客将箱包从行李架上取下放在膝上，乘务员规劝他们，但乘客不听劝告，乘务员最后采取了放任的态度。

案例分析

乘务员安全检查时，应耐心地对乘客讲明道理，告知他们这些行李在紧急情况下，会堵塞通道，严重影响撤离的速度。执行安全规定时应坚持原则，必要时可请求机组或安全员出面。否则，既可能影响其本人的安全，又可能危害其他乘客。

任务实践

（1）重点练习第一、第二段广播词，进行三段广播词客舱实练。

（2）在所给词汇后填写对应的中文或英文。

摄氏度_____   rainy season _____

华氏度_____   severe winter _____

入境和海关手续_____   ground staff _____

联程机票_____   no later than _____

航班信息系统_____   prior to _____

（3）单项选择题。

① If you are forgetful, you'd better set a(an) _____ on your phone.

    A. o'clock　　　B. reminder　　　C. remember　　　D. log

② During the flight, we will provide several beverages _____ you.

    A. with　　　B. for　　　C. to　　　D. on

③ Sorry, there is a typhoon in Xiamen. _____ is blowing hard.

    A. That　　　B. Which　　　C. Where　　　D. It

④ You can proceed directly to the departure gate _____ the gate number in flight information display system.

  A. according to   B. due to

  C. in according to   D. accord to

⑤ There is no time _____ between south Korea and Japan.

  A. changing   B. different

  C. difficulty   D. difference

（4）句子翻译。

① 地面温度为 26 摄氏度，79 华氏度。

_____

② 请您注意温度变化，适时增减衣物。

_____

③ 我们希望能再次为您服务。

_____

④ 请您至少提前 2 小时办理登机手续。

_____

⑤ 医生提醒我按时睡觉和起床。

_____

⑥ Passengers who have reserved seats on a connecting flight should reconfirm your reservation no later than 72 hours prior to the departure of the flight.

_____

⑦ Please write down the connecting fight number. I will ask our ground staff to check it.

_____

⑧ After you are cleared with immigration and Customs formalities, present the check-in baggage to the Specific Transfer Desk.

_____

⑨ Please fastened your seat-belt, secure your table, place your seat back upright, open the sunshade and switch off all the electronic devices.

_____

⑩ The local time in Tokyo is 1 hour ahead of Beijing time.

_____

（5）参考课文中的知识拓展用英文填空，并分组完成角色演练。

(Passenger X has opened the overhead compartment and taken his baggage out just before descending. flight attendant comes to stop him.)

FA: Excuse me, sir, it's required that you remain seated and keep your baggage in the overhead compartment.

PX: The purser has said we are going to descend, and I want to get ready. I am in a hurry.

FA: Sorry, sir. It's not allowed to get out the luggage before a complete stop, because _____.

PX: You are kidding. Where is the emergency? I am actually _____.

FA: Sir, it's never to be too careful. As we will arrive at the airport in about 40 minutes, it's a heavy burden for your laps and knees. _____.

PA: Okay, Okay. I will do it myself.

FA: OK, sir, thank you _____.

任务五　国际航班空中服务广播（三）
——检疫入境广播

任务导入

本任务为国际远程空中广播的最后一节，也是一个难点。本任务选取了美国、澳大利亚、法国入境检疫的相关广播三段以供大家学习。

广播要求

语速中等、吐字清晰、信息准确，起到提醒警示作用。每一段广播词都有相当多的信息要表达，既需要多次练习与矫音，也需要乘务员有丰富准确的入境检疫知识。另外，每个航班配备的入境申报表、检疫表基本都不会足量，为了减少服务沟通中的误会，建议乘务员平时多收集放在出差箱包和乘务长箱包中。

任务要求

通过本任务的学习，学习者应能熟练进行三段广播，牢记机上情景对话并演练。

一、检疫入境广播词

1. 填写美国海关申报单、入境卡

女士们、先生们：

为了缩短您在机场候机室的停留时间，现在为各位乘客播放如何填写美国移民局I-94入境卡及海关申报单，请您按照录像中的要求正确填写。

根据美国检疫规定：入境的乘客，不能随身携带新鲜水果、肉类、植物及鲜花等。如果您已带上飞机，请您在落地前自行处理或交给客舱乘务员。

我们的航班号是_____。今天是___年___月___日。填写过程中如有疑问，请随时告诉我们。我们将非常乐意地帮助您。

谢谢！

Distributing Forms (the United States)

Ladies and gentlemen,

We will be distributing the necessary forms for entry into the United States. According to the requirements of the United States Quarantine, passengers cannot bring in fresh fruit, cut flowers, plants or meats. Those passengers in possession of such items are required to dispose of them or give them to the flight attendants before arrival.

We remind you that this is _____（航空公司名称）flight _____（航班号）. Today is _____（英文具体日期）. If there is anything else we can do to make this journey more comfortable for you, please don't hesitate to call us. We are glad to serve you.

Thank you.

（注：美国I-94入境卡现已取消，但是此段广播可作为类似广播的范本。）

2. 澳大利亚入境检疫

女士们，先生们：

根据澳大利亚检疫规定，为防止口蹄疫等疫病的传入，检疫当局将进一步加大其检疫控制的力度。

凡进入澳大利亚的乘客，请严格遵守澳大利亚检疫规定，在海关申报单上填写随身携带的食品，包括肉类、奶酪、水果和其他动、植物制品的来源，或将这些物品丢置于进港通道的垃圾箱里。所有机上食品都不得带离飞机，您的行李在抵港时要接受检查。

请特别注意将您的海关申报单填写完整，虚假申报将受到处罚。

谢谢！

Australian Quarantine

Ladies and gentlemen,

Australia has intensified its strict Quarantine controls to prevent the introduction of pests and diseases such as the Foot and Mouth Virus.

To comply with Australian Quarantine regulations, declare all food items such as meat, cheese, fruit or other items of animals or plant origins on your Incoming Passenger Card. Alternatively, place these items in the bins in the arrival concourse. All aircraft food must be left on board, and your baggage will be X-rayed or screened on arrival.

Please take particular care in completing your Incoming Passenger Card, as false declarations will be punished.

Thank you!

3. 澳大利亚（法国）入境喷洒药物

女士们，先生们：

根据澳大利亚（法国）政府的要求，对所有进港飞机喷洒药物。现在由客舱乘务员对机上客舱、厕所进行药物喷洒。这些药物对人体无毒害。如您对喷洒药物有过敏反应，我们建议您在喷洒药物时用手帕捂住口鼻。

谢谢！

Spray

Ladies and gentlemen,

As the Australia/France government requires that all incoming aircrafts should be sprayed against insects, the Quarantine officer will come aboard before you deplane. The spray is non-toxic to human body, but if you are sensitive to the spray, we advise you to place your handkerchief over your nose and mouth during the spraying.

Thank you!

（注：澳大利亚和法国航班入境前客舱和货舱必须喷洒规定的药物，广播时间一般在降落致谢广播前，也就是落地前50分钟左右，由两名乘务员担任相关工作。）

词汇

distribute /dɪˈstrɪbjuːt/	vt. 分配；散布；分开；把……分类
quarantine /ˈkwɒrəntiːn/	n. 隔离；检疫；检疫区
pest /pest/	n. 害虫；有害之物
Foot and Mouth Virus	口蹄疫病毒
comply with	照做，遵守
declare /dɪˈkleə(r)/	vt. 宣布，声明；断言，宣称
	vi. 声明，宣布
origin /ˈɒrɪdʒɪn/	n. 起源；原点
concourse /ˈkɒŋkɔːs/	n. 广场；集合
particular /pəˈtɪkjələ(r)/	adj. 特别的；详细的；独有的
Incoming Passenger Card	海关申报单（也可用 Customs Declaration Form）/乘客入境登记卡（每个国家对此表格称谓不同，实质是同一种表格）
alternatively /ɔːlˈtɜːnətɪvli/	adv. 或者；要不
punish /ˈpʌnɪʃ/	vt. 惩罚；严厉对待
	vi. 惩罚
deplane /diːpleɪn/	vt. 使下飞机；从飞机上卸下
	vi. 下飞机
non-toxic /nɒnˈtɒksɪk/	adj. 无毒的
spray /spreɪ/	n. 喷雾，喷雾剂；喷雾器
	vt. 喷射
	vi. 喷
be sensitive to	对……敏感
handkerchief /ˈhæŋkətʃiːf/	n. 手帕；头巾，围巾

二、填写入境卡情景用语

1. 问询

（1）What items cannot be carried with or consigned without permission by air?

乘飞机时，哪些物品未经允许不能携带或托运？

（2）According to the "Frontier Health and Quarantine Law of The People's Republic of China", what symptoms should be consulted?

根据《中华人民共和国国境卫生检疫法》，哪些症状需要咨询？

（3）What items are not allowed to be brought into this country?

哪些物品不允许带进这个国家？

（4）What must foreign passengers declare at Customs?

外国乘客在海关必须申报什么？

2. 答疑

（1）All passengers are advised to complete the entry cards before arrival.

所有乘客均须在入境前填写入境卡。

（2）If you have unaccompanied baggage or duty-free items, please indicate this on your Customs Declaration Form.

如果您有托运的行李或免税物品，请在您的海关申报单上注明。

（3）Foreign travelers may leave with amount up to five thousand US dollars without declaration.

外国乘客最多可以携带 5000 美元的物品离开而无须申报。

词汇

consign /kənˈsaɪn/	vt. 交付；托运；寄存
frontier /ˈfrʌntɪə(r)/	n. 前沿；边界；国境
consult /kənˈsʌlt/	vt. 查阅；商量；向……请教
	vi. 请教；商议；当顾问
unaccompanied /ˌʌnəˈkʌmpənid/	adj. 无伴侣的；无伴随的
indicate /ˈɪndɪkeɪt/	vt. 表明；指出

句型

（1）According to the requirements of the United States Quarantine, ...

根据美国检疫要求，……

（2）Those passengers in possession of such items...

携带此类物品的乘客……

（3）To comply with Australian Quarantine regulations, ...

　　　为遵守（符合）澳大利亚检疫规定，……

（4）Please take particular care in completing your Incoming Passenger Card.

　　　请特别留意入境申报单的填写。

（5）What items are not allowed to be brought into this country?

　　　哪些物品不允许带进这个国家？

知识拓展：填写入境卡

机上入境卡配备数量不够，但恰巧乘客需要，乘务人员应如何说明？

案例分析

首先应向乘客致歉，讲明原因，并告知下机后可以在入境柜台处填写。有些转机乘客赶时间，可以在落地前 30 分钟请带班乘务长或客舱经理要求机长通知驻地代办，在航班落地后机门廊桥外帮助发放。

任 务 实 践

（1）重点练习第一、第二段广播词，进行三段广播词客舱实练。

（2）在所给词汇后填写对应的中文或英文。

　　虚假申报_____　　quarantine regulation _____

　　无毒害的_____　　in possession of _____

　　入境申报单_____　　dispose of _____

　　口蹄疫病毒_____　　unaccompanied minors _____

　　海关申报单_____　　arrival concourse _____

（3）单项选择题。

① The company has _____ its strict controls to manage the staff.

　　A. intensified　　　　　　　　B. extended

　　C. intended　　　　　　　　　D. esterified

② Your baggage will be X-rayed or screened _____.

　　A. on arrival　　　　　　　　 B. upon arrival

　　C. when you arrive　　　　　 D. All the above

③ Please take particular care in _____ your application form.

   A. complete   B. completing   C. competing   D. compiling

④ All incoming aircrafts should be sprayed _____ insects.

   A. with   B. to   C. for   D. against

⑤ Foreign travelers may leave with _____ up to 5000 US dollars without declaration.

   A. amount   B. mount   C. account   D. number

（4）句子翻译。

① 如果您有随身行李或免税物品，请在您的海关申报单上注明。

② 乘坐国际航班时，活体动物和植物未经允许不能携带或托运。

③ 在英国，请遵守交通规则，左侧通行。

④ 工作时，要特别留意自己的笑容。

⑤ 外国乘客在海关必须申报什么？

⑥ If you are sensitive to the seafood, we advise you to get away from it and take some other food.

⑦ All passengers are advised to complete the entry cards before arrival.

⑧ Alternatively, you can place these items in the bins in the arrival concourse.

⑨ We will be distributing the necessary forms for entry into Sweden.

⑩ We should intensify our measures to prevent the introduction of diseases such as COVID-19.

（5）参考课文中的知识拓展用英文填空，并分组完成角色演练。

(Passenger P is travelling to UK and she needs the entry card.)

PX: Hi, Miss, I am travelling to UK. Shall I complete any forms?

FA: Yes, madam, _____. Moreover, if you have unaccompanied baggage or duty-free items, _____.

PX: You mean that I need an _____ and a Customs Declaration Form?

FA: Yes. I will bring you the forms, OK?

PX: OK, thank you.

(several minutes later)

FA: Sorry, madam, the forms onboard have been handed out.

PA: Oh, so what? What shall I do?

FA: _____, madam. The forms are _____ at Immigration Counter, where you can complete the forms. As you are travelling to UK, I think you may have sufficient time to do that.

PA: OK, I think so. Thank you.

任务六　国际航班落地滑行广播

任务导入

本任务广播相对比较基础，摘选了悉尼航班落地广播，因为悉尼航班落地转机航班和出口比较容易混淆，需要播报准确，给转机乘客提示清楚。

广播要求

语速中等、咬字清晰；语气亲切、信息准确。第一段和第二段广播基本相似，但由于悉尼转机乘客的特殊性，进行针对练习。第三段广播一般情况下用不到，只有在远机位，天气恶劣的情况下会用到，可以做了解和参考。

任务要求

通过本任务的学习，学习者应能熟练进行第一段广播，牢记机上情景对话并演练。

一、落地滑行广播

1. 国际航班落地

尊敬的各位乘客：

飞机已经降落在_____国际机场。现在是当地时间____点____分。外面温度____摄氏度，____华氏度。

（由于天气原因，延误了本次航班，耽误了您的旅行，对此我们深表歉意。）

飞机还将继续滑行，在"系好安全带"指示灯熄灭之前请您不要开启手机电源或关闭飞行模式，请不要离开自己的座位。打开行李架时请您小心，以防止行李滑落发生意外。

下机时，请带好您的护照、证件以及全部手提物品到候机厅办理入境和海关手续，您所交运的行李请到行李提取处领取。需要转机的乘客请到候机厅转机柜台办理手续。

继续前往_____的乘客，①下机时请凭机票或登机牌向地面人员换取过站登机牌；_____航班中转的旅客②请在飞机上休息等候。飞机将在本站停留_____（时间）。

各位乘客，感谢您选择_____航空，本次航班与_____实施代码共享，感谢_____会员再次乘坐_____航空班机。

我们期待着再次与您相会。

谢谢！

After Landing (International Long haul)

Ladies and gentlemen,

We have just landed at _____ airport where the local time is _____. The ground temperature is _____ degree(s) centigrade or _____ degree(s) Fahrenheit.

(Once again, we do sincerely apologize for the delay of our flight. Thank you for your patience and understanding.)

It is safety requirement that you remain seated and the seat-belt fastened, and keep your phone off or in flight mode until the aircraft has come to a complete stop and the "Fasten Seat-belt" sign is off. Please take care when opening the overhead compartments so that items inside do not fall out.

Please make sure to take your passport, certificates and belongings with you when deplaning. Entry and customs formalities will be completed in the terminal. Your checked baggage may be claimed at the baggage claim area.

Transit passengers please proceed to the transfer counters in the terminal to arrange for your connecting flight.

Passengers continuing to _____ ① are requested to get your transit boarding pass from the ground staff; _____ ② please remain on board.

Thank you for choosing _____ Airlines/Airways which is code share with _____. For members of _____（航空联盟/航空俱乐部）, thanks for flying with us again. We are looking forward to seeing you again soon.

Thank you!

2. 悉尼航班落地

女士们、先生们：

飞机已经到达悉尼国际机场。现在是当地时间_____，外面温度_____摄氏度、_____华氏度飞机还将继续滑行，在"系好安全带"指示灯熄灭之前请您不要开启手机电源或关闭飞行模式，请不要离开自己的座位。打开行李架时请您小心，以防止行李滑落发生意外。

乘坐澳大利亚快达航空公司QF399或399以内航班号的乘客，下机后请按照候机楼内的指示，直接办理转机手续，托运行李不需要提取。

乘坐快达航空公司QF400或400以上航班号的乘客，办完入境手续后，您必须提取所有的交运行李并通过澳大利亚海关的检查，然后办理转机手续。

各位乘客，感谢您选择_____航空，本次航班与_____实施代码共享，感谢_____会员再次乘坐_____班机，我们期待着再次与您相会。

谢谢！

Landing at Sydney Airport

Ladies and gentlemen,

We have landed at Sydney International Airport. The local time is _____. The ground temperature is _____ degree(s) centigrade or _____ degree(s) Fahrenheit.

It is a safety requirement that you remain seated and the seat-belt fastened and keep your phone off or in flight mode until the aircraft has come to a complete stop and the "Fasten Seat-belt" sign is off. Please take care when opening the overhead compartments so that the items inside do not fall out.

Transit passengers who take Qantas Airways flight QF399 or below please go directly to the transfer counter according to the signboard in the terminal.

While transit passengers who take Qantas Airways flight QF400 or above please proceed to the transfer counter after the completion of your entry and Customs formalities in the terminal.

Ladies and gentlemen, thank you for choosing _____ Airlines which is code share with _____. For members of _____, thanks for flying with us again and we hope to see you again.

Thank you!

3. 开机门前提醒

各位乘客：

（1）现在外面正在下雨/下雪，请您准备好雨具，地面湿滑，请您小心脚下。

（2）现在外面正在下雨/下雪，我们的地面工作人员将为您发放雨衣，地面湿滑，请您小心脚下。

Reminder

Ladies and gentlemen,

（1）It's raining/snowing outside, please prepare your umbrella or raincoat and watch your step(s) when deplaning.

（2）It's raining/snowing outside, so the ground is slippery. Please watch your step when deplaning. Raincoats are available at the exits.

词汇

sincerely /sɪnˈsɪəli/	adv. 真诚地；由衷地，诚恳地
apologize /əˈpɒlədʒaɪz/	vi. 道歉，谢罪；辩解，辩护
Fasten Seat-belt sign	"系好安全带"指示灯
certificate /səˈtɪfɪkət/	n. 证书；文凭，合格证书
belonging /bɪˈlɒŋɪŋ/	n. 所有物，附属物
formality /fɔːˈmæləti/	n. 礼节；仪式；正式手续
signboard /ˈsaɪnbɔːd/	n. 招牌，告示牌，广告牌
slippery /ˈslɪpəri/	adj. 滑的；不稳定的

二、航班抵达情景用语

1. 抵达前向乘客道别

We will be landing very soon.

我们马上就要降落了。

Hope you enjoyed the flight.

希望您度过了一个愉快的航程。

Thank you for flying with us.

感谢您乘坐我们的航班。

Hope to see you again soon.

希望能很快再见到您。

Enjoy your stay in Shanghai.

希望您在上海过得愉快。

Please use front door for disembarkation.

下飞机时请走前门。

2. 为乘客取回衣物

Here is your overcoat.

这是您的外套。

It's very cold outside. May I suggest you put on the overcoat.

外面很冷。建议您穿上外套。

词汇

disembarkation /ˌdɪsˌembɑːˈkeɪʃn/　　n. 下（车、船、飞机等）

overcoat /ˈəʊvəkəʊt/　　n. 大衣，外套

句型

（1）It is safety requirement that you (should)...

根据安全要求，您需要（做）……

（2）...until the aircraft has come to a complete stop.

……直到飞机完全停稳。

（3）..., when opening the overhead compartments so that items inside do not fall out.

当（您）打开行李架时……，以便（里面的）行李不会掉落。

（4）Passengers continuing to Canberra /kænb(ə)rə/ are requested to...

继续前往堪培拉的乘客，请您（您被要求去做）……

（5）Raincoats are available at the exits.

雨衣位于（可获得并使用）出口处。

知识拓展：国际航班转机

洛杉矶航班乘客询问乘务员航班到达之后还要转机，托运行李是否要取出？

案例分析

根据美国海关规定，无论乘客的目的地是美国还是其他地方，都必须在到达美国的第一站取出所有的行李，接受美国海关的检查。若乘客还想了解其他详细的情况，乘务员可建议乘客到达洛杉矶后与他们的办事处人员联系或者航班落地前 30 分钟请机长通知地面人员到廊桥口引导转机乘客。正常情况下外站办事处工作人员都会在国际远程到站前在廊桥等候（见图 3-5）。

图 3-5

任务实践

（1）重点练习第一段广播词，进行三段广播词客舱实练。

（2）在所给词汇后填写对应的中文或英文。

登机牌_____　　local time _____

地面温度_____　　transit passengers _____

"系好安全带"指示灯_____　　overhead compartments _____

候机厅转机柜台_____　　checked baggage _____

代码共享_____　　electronic devices _____

（3）单项选择题。

① We have just landed at Sydney International Airport where the _____ time is 4:30 p.m.

A. local　　　　B. logical　　　　C. legal　　　　D. locate

② It's required that all the passengers _____ onboard, waiting for taking off.
   A. remained   B. remain
   C. should remain   D. remaining

③ Your checked baggage may be _____ at the baggage _____ area.
   A. claim; claimed   B. claimed; claim
   C. claim; claim   D. claimed; claimed

④ We are looking forward to _____ you in China.
   A. meeting   B. meet   C. meet with   D. meeting with

⑤ Please remain seated _____ the aircraft comes to a complete stop.
   A. while   B. not until   C. until   D. when

（4）句子翻译。

① "系好安全带"指示灯熄灭之前，请不要离开自己的座位；在飞机完全停稳之前，请您不要开启手机电源。

② 下飞机时请您小心慢行，以防滑倒摔伤。

③ 本次航班与东方航空实施代码共享。

④ 请务必带好您的护照、证件和随身物品。

⑤ 我们期盼再次与您相聚在云端。

⑥ Please use front door for disembarkation.

⑦ Entry and customs formalities will be completed in the terminal.

⑧ Please take care when opening the overhead compartments so that the items inside do not fall out.

⑨ Transit passengers please proceed to the transfer counters in the terminal to arrange for your connecting flight.

⑩ It's raining outside, so the ground is slippery. Please watch your step when deplaning.

_____

（5）参考课文中的知识拓展用英文填空，并分组完成角色演练。

(The aircraft has landed at Bangkok. Passenger B transferring to another country is asking for help after the complete stop.)

FA: Hi, madam, may I help you?

PX: I am going to Colombo /kəˈlʌmbəu/, Sri Lanka /ʃriːˈlɑːŋkə/, how can I find the flight I should take?

FA: Well, madam, we are arriving at Bangkok where you cannot go straight to Sri Lanka, you should apply the transit visa. So please proceed to _____ to arrange for _____.

PX: OK, but where is the transfer counter?

FA: You can follow the _____ which can lead you to the transfer counter. Or, you can ask the staff for direction.

PX: OK, I see, thank you very much.

FA: _____.

本项目教学音频

项目四

特情广播教学

项目目标

知识目标	掌握起飞延误广播的英语生词和句型； 掌握落地延误广播的英语生词和句型； 掌握特殊事件广播的英语生词和句型； 掌握落地延误的英语生词和句型。
技能目标	流利地进行起飞延误广播及情景对话； 流利地进行落地延误广播及情景对话； 流利地进行特殊事件广播及情景对话； 流利地进行落地延误及情景对话。
职业素养目标	培养学生爱岗敬业的精神； 培养学生机上广播职业素养； 培养学生对旅客的主动服务意识； 培养学生航班应急处置能力和灵活应对的服务能力。

任务一　起飞延误广播

任务导入

从本项目开始，我们将进入特殊情况广播的学习。特殊情况广播简称"特情广播"。本任务从航班起飞前的延误情况中选择了四种常见情况供大家学习。

广播要求

语速中等、咬字清晰；语气委婉诚恳。本任务每段广播基本相似，只是延误的原因不同，要让乘客听到延误信息以及歉意。此种广播之前乘务员必须和带班乘务长/客舱经理确认好延误播报信息，不要随意播报。

任务要求

通过本任务的学习，学习者应牢记延误高频词汇和句型并能灵活运用。

一、起飞延误广播词

➡ 1. 航空管制原因 ⬅

女士们、先生们：

由于航空管制原因，我们暂时还无法确认飞机起飞时间，请您在座位上休息等候。如有进一步消息，我们会立刻通知您。（在此期间，我们将为您提供餐饮服务。）

对于给各位带来的不便，我们深表歉意，并感谢大家合作。

➡ Air Traffic Control ⬅

Ladies and gentlemen,

We haven't been informed about the time of departure from air traffic control. Please remain seated and wait for a moment. We will keep you informed.(We will be serving food/beverages during this period.)

Your understanding will be much appreciated.

（注：一般航班延误 30 分钟左右航空公司会提供饮料，因为塔台尚未给出时间，所以会先赠送一遍饮料。）

➡ 2. 机械原因 ⬅

女士们、先生们：

由于飞机机械故障，我们不能按时起飞，为了确保飞行安全，机务维修人员正在积极排除故障。如有进一步的消息，我们将及时通知您。

对于给各位带来的不便，我们深表歉意，并感谢大家合作。

➡ Mechanical Reason ⬅

Ladies and gentlemen,

Due to the aircraft mechanical problem(s), we will wait _____ minutes for maintenance to solve the problem. Please remain seated and we will keep you informed.

Your understanding will be much appreciated.

➡ 3. 等待货物 / 行李装载 ⬅

女士们、先生们：

由于飞机货物 / 行李还未装载完毕，我们还需等待_____分钟才能起飞，请您在座位上休息等候。

对于给各位带来的不便，我们深表歉意，并感谢大家合作。

➡ Loading of Cargo ⬅

Ladies and gentlemen,

　　Due to the loading of cargo/luggage, we will wait _____ minutes to take off. Please remain seated and we will keep you informed.

　　Your understanding will be much appreciated.

➡ 4. 飞机 / 跑道除冰 / 除雪 ⬅

女士们、先生们：

　　由于飞机 / 跑道需除冰 / 除雪，我们不能按时起飞。请您在座位上休息等候。对于给各位带来的不便，我们深表歉意，并感谢大家合作。

➡ Deicing ⬅

Ladies and gentlemen,

　　Due to the aircraft/runway deicing, we have to wait a few minutes to take off. Please remain seated and we will keep you informed.

　　Your understanding will be much appreciated.

（注：除雪、除冰一般需要十几分钟时间，之后就是重新排队起飞，所以用 a few minutes。）

词汇

air traffic control	空中交通管制
appreciate /əˈpriːʃieɪt/	vt. 欣赏；感激
solve the problem	解决问题
luggage /ˈlʌɡɪdʒ/	n. 行李；皮箱
deice /ˈdaɪs/	vt. 除冰；防止结冰

二、起飞延误情景用语

1. 询问延误情况

（1）We will wait until a take-off clearance is given, owing to the air traffic control.

　　由于交通管制，我将一直等到发放起飞许可才可以起飞。

（2）When shall we take off? I have a very important meeting at two p.m.

飞机什么时候可以起飞呢？我下午两点有个很重要的会议。

（3）Our departure time will be delayed for about half an hour. The delay shouldn't be too extensive.

预计起飞时间将被推迟30分钟，本次延误将不会太久。

2. 解释延误原因

（1）The flight has been delayed because of bad weather.

由于天气恶劣，航班延误。

（2）The airport of our destination has been closed. The reason is unknown at the moment.

目的地机场已关闭。关闭原因尚不确定

（3）We have to divert to Guangzhou airport due to heavy rain in the Shenzhen area.

由于深圳地区大雨，我们不得不改飞广州机场。

词汇

clearance /ˈklɪərəns/	n. 清除；准许；（飞机起降的）许可
extensive /ɪkˈstensɪv/	adj. 广泛的；大量的；广阔的
destination /ˌdestɪˈneɪʃn/	n. 目的地，终点

句型

（1）Owing to the air traffic control,...

由于航空管制，……

（2）We have to divert to Guangzhou airport.

我们不得不改飞广州机场。

知识拓展：航班延误

航班（见图4-1）没有起飞，乘客向乘务员抱怨"什么延误时间无法确定，一拖再拖？"

案例分析

1. 天气原因

由于天气原因而导致航班延误乘务员应向乘客道歉，没能一次性提供最确切的信息，并恳请乘客相信，作为航空公司也最希望能迅速地在航班延误时，第一时间内将

图 4-1

准确的延误时间通知到各位乘客。但航班延误是由于天气原因造成的，机组只能根据气象部门提供的资料了解飞机在短时间内还无法安全起降，所以不得不根据实际情况的变化推迟航班起飞的原因和时间。

2. 机械故障

如果是由于机械故障而导致航班延误时，乘务员向乘客道歉，没能一次性提供最确切的信息，并恳请乘客相信，作为航空公司也最希望能迅速地在航班延误第一时间内将准确的延误时间通知到各位乘客。但航班延误是由于飞机故障造成的，在排除故障前，维修人员对故障的排除时间只能作一个大致的估计。在故障排除过程中，随着新的问题和情况的出现，可能超出原先的估计，再次向乘客解释机务人员现正在全力抢修，一旦飞机修好，即刻广播通知起飞。

任务实践

（1）熟读四段广播词，进行客舱广播实练。

（2）在所给词汇后填写对应的中文或英文。

航空管制＿＿＿＿＿＿＿＿　　the time of departure ＿＿＿＿＿＿＿＿
起飞许可＿＿＿＿＿＿＿＿　　loading of cargo ＿＿＿＿＿＿＿＿
大雨＿＿＿＿＿＿＿＿　　runway deicing ＿＿＿＿＿＿＿＿
塔台＿＿＿＿＿＿＿＿　　owing to ＿＿＿＿＿＿＿＿
半个小时＿＿＿＿＿＿＿＿　　divert to ＿＿＿＿＿＿＿＿

（3）单项选择题。

① The flight will be delayed ＿＿＿＿ half an hour.

  A. for   B. at   C. with   D. to

② _____ the aircraft mechanical problems, we will wait 40 minutes.

　　A. Due to　　　　　　　　　　　　B. Owing to

　　C. Because of　　　　　　　　　　D. All of the above

③ Your cooperation will be _____ appreciated.

　　A. very　　　　　　　　　　　　　B. too

　　C. much　　　　　　　　　　　　　D. more

④ We will wait until _____ is given.

　　A. a take off clearance　　　　　　B. a take-off clearance

　　C. take-off clearance　　　　　　　D. take off clearance

⑤ The road to the airport is _____ and the reason is _____ at the moment.

　　A. closed; unknown　　　　　　　　B. closing; unknown

　　C. closing; unknowing　　　　　　　D. closed; unknowing

（4）句子翻译。

① 由于交通管制，我们需要等待，直至得到起飞许可。

_____

② 非常感谢您的理解与合作。

_____

③ We will wait 30 minutes for maintenance to solve the mechanical problem.

_____

④ We have to divert to Chongqing Airport due to heavy rain in the Xi'an area.

_____

⑤ We will be serving beverages during this period.

_____

（5）参考知识拓展用英文填空，并分组完成角色演练。

(Passenger S is complaining the delay of the flight.)

PX: How long do we have to wait? I have an important meeting this afternoon.

FA: Sorry to keep you waiting, sir. Due to _____, our flight haven't got the take-off clearance.

PX: I don't care what reason. When to go?

FA: Sir, I know the delay get you in anxiety, but the safety always comes first, right? The air traffic control is taking the whole into consideration.

PA: I am in a hurry for my meeting, a very important meeting. I ask to speak to the Captain.

FA: I can understand your feeling, sir. But the captain is waiting for the take-off clearance. Once the clearance is given, the captain will make an announcement for take-off.

Please wait a few minutes, I think _____.

PX: Waiting, waiting, waiting.

FA: Yes, sir. We all have to wait. May I bring some beverage, newspapers or magazines for you?

PX: Okay, some newspapers.

FA: Thank you for _____.

任务二　落地延误广播

任务导入

上个任务介绍了起飞延误的四种情况，本任务介绍落地的三种情况，可以结合案例比较学习。

广播要求

语速中等、咬字清晰；语气委婉诚恳，要让乘客听到延误信息以及歉意，强调乘客不要离开座位等内容要读重音。

任务要求

通过本任务的学习，学习者应牢记延误高频词汇和句型并能灵活运用。

一、落地延误广播词

1. 机场的客梯车 / 摆渡车 / 廊桥未到

女士们、先生们：

由于_____机场的客梯车 / 摆渡车（见图 4-2）/ 廊桥没有及时到位，我们暂时还不能下飞机，请您在座位上休息等候。

对于给各位带来的不便，我们深表歉意，并感谢大家的合作。

图 4-2

Airport Shuttle Delay

Ladies and gentlemen,

We regret to inform that you cannot deplane at the moment since the shuttle bus to the terminal / the bridge hasn't been in position. Please remain seated and we will keep you informed.

Your understanding will be much appreciated.

2. 移民局 / 海关人员未到

女士们、先生们：

由于移民局 / 海关人员未到，我们暂时还不能下机，请您在座位上休息等候。

对于给各位带来的不便，我们深表歉意，并感谢大家合作。

Immigration/Customs Officer Delay

Ladies and gentlemen,

We regret to inform that you cannot deplane at the moment since the immigration/Customs officer has not arrived yet. Please remain seated and we will keep you informed.

Your understanding will be much appreciated.

3. 乘客在机内等候飞机加油

女士们、先生们：

我们的飞机正在加油，为了安全，请您在座位上坐好，不要吸烟，不要使用手机，并且不要系上安全带。

谢谢！

➤ Refueling (with Passengers on Board) ⬅

Ladies and gentlemen,

　　The aircraft is now being refueled. It is safety requirement that you remain seated, unfasten your seat-belt, avoid using mobile phones, and refrain from smoking.

　　Thank you!

　　（注：此段广播一般是用于国内多段航班，有乘客到终点，但是中转站不下飞机，飞机在中转机场加油时播报。）

词汇

shuttle /ˈʃʌtl/	n. 穿梭；穿梭班机、公共汽车等
delay /dɪˈleɪ/	v. 延期；耽搁
	n. 延期；耽搁；被耽搁或推迟的时间
terminal /ˈtɜːmɪnl/	n. 航空站；终点站；航站楼
	adj. 末端的；终点的
immigration /ˌɪmɪˈɡreɪʃn/	n. 外来移民；移居；入境

二、中转乘客延误情景用语

（1）Sir, we've got the information about your connecting flight from our ground staff. Your flight will start boarding at Gate Fifteen. Luckily it's in the same terminal. And we'll be landing at 9:20 p.m., that means you have fifty minutes to do the transfer. It's a little bit tight but I think you can still catch it.

　　先生，我们刚得知了您的转机信息。您的后续航班会在同一个航站楼的 15 号登机门登机。我们的航班会在晚上 9 点 20 分落地，也就是您将有 50 分钟用于中转。虽然时间有点紧，但我认为您还能赶得上。不过动作快点应该没问题。

（2）Sir, I'm sorry you've missed your connecting flight. But don't worry, we will contact our ground staff to help you to catch the next available flight.

　　先生，对不起，您已经错过后续航班。但请别着急，我们会联系地面人员帮您去转下一班可以乘坐的航班。

（3）Next time when you need to catch a transit flight after such a long distance flight, may I suggest you leave at least two hours between them.

下一次当您需要像这样一个长途飞行后转机时,建议您在两个航班之间预留至少 2 个小时的时间。

词汇

transfer /trænsˈfɜː(r)/　　v. 移交;转移(地方);(使)换乘
　　　　　　　　　　　　n.(地点的)转移;权力的移交;(公共汽车、飞机等的)转移
catch /kætʃ/　　　　　　　vt. & vi. 赶上;抓住
a transit flight　　　　　　中转航班
a long distance flight　　长途飞行

句型

(1) We regret to inform you that...
我们抱歉地通知您……

(2) You cannot deplane at the moment since the bridge hasn't been in position.
因为廊桥还没就位,所以您还不能下飞机。

(3) Avoid using mobile phones.
不要使用手机。

(4) Please remain seated and we will keep you informed.
请您(保持)坐好(状态),我们将及时告知您(相关信息)。

(5) Next time when you need to...
下一次当您需要……

知识拓展:延误转机

乘客在落地前询问乘务员:"我后面还要转接其他航班,你们的航班延误将导致我坐不上后续航班怎么办?万一我赶不上后续航班,我的托运行李怎么办?"

案例分析

乘务员首先向乘客表示歉意,请乘客下机后与到达站的办事处(代理)人员联系,他们会为乘客安排其他合适的航班,机组也会把所有转机乘客的姓名、转接航班和行李情况通知到达站做后续安排。

任务实践

（1）熟读三段广播词，进行客舱广播实练。

（2）在所给词汇后填写对应的中文或英文。

地面工作人员 _____   airport shuttle _____

移民局工作人员 _____   in position _____

禁止吸烟 _____   deplane _____

十五号门 _____   at the moment _____

长航线航班 _____   at least _____

（3）单项选择题。

① We regret _____ that you cannot get onboard.
   A. to inform   B. informing   C. informed   D. inform

② The aircraft is now _____.
   A. been refueled   B. refueling   C. being refueled   D. refueled

③ In such situation, you'd better avoid _____.
   A. angry   B. getting angry   C. getting anger   D. angrying

④ _____, the shuttle bus has arrived in time.
   A. Luck   B. Lucky   C. Luckily   D. Unlucky

⑤ I am going to catch _____ long distance flight, so boring!
   A. so   B. such   C. so a   D. such a

（4）句子翻译。

① 您还不能下飞机，因为移民局工作人员还没到。

② 时间有点紧张，但我相信，您还是能够赶得上的。

③ 非常感谢您的理解。

④ 对不起，您已经赶不上这次航班了。

⑤ 我们刚刚从地面服务人员那里得知您的转机航班的相关消息。

⑥ We regret to inform that you cannot deplane at the moment since the shuttle bus to the terminal hasn't been in position.

⑦ Please remain seated and we will keep you informed.

_____

⑧ We will contact our ground staff to help you to catch the next available flight.

_____

⑨ We'll be landing at 9:20 p.m., that means you have fifty minutes to do the transfer.

_____

⑩ It is safety requirement that you remain seated, unfasten your seat-belt, avoid using mobile phones, and refrain from smoking.

_____

（5）参考课文中的知识拓展用英文填空，并分组完成角色演练。

(Passenger F is complaining about the delay of the flight due to the airbridge not in position.)

PX: Hey! When to get off? I have my transferring flight at 12:30p.m..

FA: Sorry, sir. I'm afraid that _____.

PX: What makes it not in position? Does your airline owe money to the airport?

FA: Sir, sorry to keep you waiting, especially when you have a connecting flight. I can understand the delay may make you in anxiety. But please don't worry, _____.

PX: A bit tight? You think? But what if I miss the flight? What about my consigned baggage?

FA: Don't worry, sir. If you miss your flight, _____.

PA: Wish so.

FA: _____.

任务三　特殊事件广播

任务导入

本任务精选了广播寻找医护人员、失物招领、飞机颠簸和备降四类比较有代表性的广播供大家学习，其他类型的事件可以参照此四类广播。本任务的寻找医护人员可以加入机上医疗急救的课程中学习。

广播要求

语速中等偏快、咬字清晰，起到提醒作用，备降广播态度要诚恳。本任务每段内容都不同，为各种突发情况下的广播起到模板和借鉴的作用。第四段广播之前乘务员必须和带班乘务长/客舱经理确认好延误播报信息，不要随意播报；而飞机颠簸广播，"系好安全带灯"一亮出就要进行客舱广播，建议背诵。

任务要求

本任务课程能使学习者背诵出颠簸广播，学会使用其他三种特情广播，并灵活使用。

一、特殊事件广播词

1. 寻找医护人员

女士们、先生们：

现在机上有一位病人（即将分娩的孕妇）需要医疗帮助，如果您是医生或护理人员，请马上与乘务员联系。

谢谢！

Medical Assistance

Ladies and gentlemen,

May I have your attention, please.

We have a passenger in need of medical attention. (A lady is going to give birth to a baby.) Would any medical personnel onboard please identify yourself to the flight attendants immediately.

Thank you!

2. 失物认领

女士们、先生们：

我们在候机楼____号安全检查口/客舱内（前/中/后舱）洗手间里找到_____。如果是您遗失的，请及时与乘务员联系。

谢谢！

（注：不要透露失物的具体特征，以便认领时让失主自我描述）

Property Found

Ladies and gentlemen,

May I have your attention please.

A/an _____ has been found at the No. _____ security inspection counter in the terminal/in the cabin/in the lavatory (of front/middle/rear cabin).

If there is a passenger who has lost, please identify yourself to the flight attendants immediately.

Thank you!

3. 寻找失物

女士们、先生们：

有位乘客在前（中、后）舱/洗手间遗失了_____。如有哪位乘客拾到，请及时与乘务员联系。我们谨代表失主向您表示感谢。

Property Lost

Ladies and gentlemen,

May I have your attention, please.

We have a passenger who has lost a/an _____ in the _____ (front/middle/rear section/lavatory). If anyone has found this _____, please contact our flight attendants.

Thank you!

4. 飞机颠簸

女士们、先生们：

现在飞机正在颠簸，请您在座位上坐好，系紧安全带，在"系好安全带"指示灯熄灭之前不要离开座位，不要使用洗手间。（在这段时间里，我们将暂停客舱服务。）

谢谢！

Turbulence

Ladies and gentlemen,

We are experiencing (a little) turbulence. It is safety requirement that you return to your seat and fasten your seat-belt. Please also avoid using the toilets at this time.(Cabin service will be suspended during this period.)

Thank you!

5. 备降

女士们、先生们：

（1）由于＿＿＿＿机场（天气原因、大雾、罢工、机场关闭、跑道上有障碍物一时无法消除）；

（2）由于机上有一位患者 / 一位即将分娩的孕妇；

（3）由于航路有雷雨，本架飞机将不能正常降落在＿＿＿＿机场；

（4）由于航路强顶风，本架飞机将不能继续往前飞行，需要加燃油；

（5）由于飞机机械故障（一台发动机发生故障，请各位乘客不要惊慌），机长决定在＿＿＿＿机场备降，大约在＿＿＿＿（一般为30分钟）分钟后到达＿＿＿＿机场。对于本次航班不能正常到达＿＿＿＿机场，我们深表歉意。

感谢您的谅解！

Additional Stop

Ladies and gentlemen,

(1) Due to bad weather/a strike/a runway obstruction at ＿＿＿＿ airport, it has been closed.

(2) A passenger in need of medical attention. (A lady is going to give childbirth.)

(3) Due to the heavy thunderstorm ahead of us.

(4) Due to strong head-winds, we will have to make a fuel stop.

(5) Due to the left (right) engine has a mechanical problem, our captain has decided to make an additional stop. We are going to land at ＿＿＿＿ airport in half an hour. Further information will be given to you after landing.

We apologize for the inconvenience caused and thank you for your understanding.

词汇

in need of	需要；缺少；须要；必要
medical attention/ assistance	医疗援助
medical personnel	医护人员
identify oneself	证明自己的身份
rear /rɪə(r)/	n. 后面
	adj. 后方的，后面的；背面的
lavatory /ˈlævətri/	n. 厕所
property /ˈprɒpəti/	n. 财产；所有权

contact /ˈkɒntækt/	n. 接触，联系
	vt.& vi. 使接触，联系
turbulence /ˈtɜːbjələns/	n. 湍流，骚乱，动荡
toilet /ˈtɔɪlət/	n. 厕所
suspend /səˈspend/	vt. 延缓，推迟；使暂停
strike /straɪk/	n. 罢工
runway /ˈrʌnweɪ/	n. 跑道；河床；滑道
obstruction /əbˈstrʌkʃn/	n. 障碍；阻碍；妨碍
childbirth /ˈtʃaɪldbɜːθ/	n. 分娩
thunderstorm /ˈθʌndəstɔːm/	n. (气象)雷暴；雷暴雨；大雷雨
head-wind	顶头风，顶风
make an additional stop	备降

二、特殊事件情景用语

1. 遭遇气流时

Please fasten your seat-belt.

请系好安全带。

The seat-belt sign is on. Please return to your seat.

安全带灯亮了，请您回座位坐好。

2. 客舱巡视

The lavatory is at the rear of the cabin.

洗手间在座舱的后面。

The lavatory is occupied right now.

洗手间现在有人。

3. 乘客健康问题

（1）How do you feel?

您感觉怎么样？

Would you like to take a rest?

您需要休息一下吗？

Please take a rest. You can call me if you need help.

您休息一下，如果有需要可以叫我。

（2）Do you need medicine?

　　您需要药吗?

　　Have you got any medicine with you?

　　请问您自己备药了吗?

　　Are you allergic to any medicine?

　　您对药物过敏吗?

（3）Do you have asthma?

　　您有哮喘吗?

　　Do you have high blood pressure?

　　您有高血压吗?

词汇

occupy /ˈɒkjupaɪ/	vt. 占据，占领
medicine /ˈmedɪsn/	n. 药
be allergic /əˈlɜːdʒɪk/ to	对……过敏
asthma /ˈæsmə/	n. 哮喘，气喘
high blood pressure	高血压

句型

（1）May I have your attention, please.
　　请注意。

（2）We have a passenger in need of medical attention.
　　我们的一位乘客需要医疗帮助（一位需要医疗帮助的乘客）。

（3）Please identify yourself to the flight attendants.
　　请向乘务员表明（证明）您的身份。

（4）Cabin service will be suspended during this period.
　　在此期间，客舱服务将会暂停。

（5）We apologize for the inconvenience caused by...
　　由……造成的不便，我们深表歉意。

知识拓展：飞行关键阶段特情案例

某航班，飞机快放起落架（见图4-3）时，一位乘客突然呕吐，需要一杯温开水。碰巧后舱矿泉水已用完。考虑到乘客急需，乘务员立即从烧水箱接了一杯开水提供给她，乘客无心理准备，喝水时烫了舌头，表示强烈不满。

图 4-3

案例分析

为了自身和他人的安全，乘务员应该待飞机着陆后再给乘客提供水。乘客呕吐或吃药时应供应矿泉水或温开水。

任务实践

（1）熟读三段广播词，进行客舱广播实练。

（2）在所给词汇后填写对应的中文或英文。

证明自己的身份_____   medical assistance_____

强顶风_____   give birth to _____

安检口_____   mechanical problem _____

医护人员_____   further information _____

客舱服务_____   be allergic to _____

（3）单项选择题。

① If you want to claim the lost things, you should _____ to the staff.

    A. identify   B. identify yourself

    C. identification   D. your identification

② When you _____, you can call me or my colleagues.

    A. are in need of help   B. need help

    C. are needing help   D. Both A and B

③ The witness who has clues please _____ the police.

    A. connect   B. contact   C. touch   D. link

④ We apologize for the inconvenience _____ by the delay.

    A. caused   B. due to   C. because   D. because of

⑤ Excuse me, madam, are you allergic _____ any medicine?

    A. to   B. of   C. with   D. at

（4）句子翻译。

① 我们正在遭遇轻微颠簸，请您回到自己的座位上，并系好安全带。

② 我们在候机楼22号安检口捡到一件灰色外套。

③ 在此期间，客舱服务将会暂停。

④ 有乘客在客舱中部丢失手套一副，有捡到者请与乘务人员联系。

⑤ 飞机降落后，我们将向您通报详细信息。

⑥ Would any medical personnel onboard please identify yourself to the flight attendants immediately.

⑦ Ladies and gentlemen, may I have your attention, please.

⑧ If there is a passenger who has lost please contact us soon.

⑨ Due to strong head-winds, we will have to make a fuel stop.

⑩ Due to the left engine has a mechanical problem, our captain has decided to make an additional stop.

（5）参考课文中的知识拓展用英文填空，并分组完成角色演练。

(Passenger Y is airsick, in need of water.)

FA: Excuse me, sir, anything I do for you?

PX: I am airsick now, _____.

FA: OK, just a minute.

PX: Hush! Too hot! My tongue hurts!

FA: Sorry, sir. I do apologize _____.

PA: Why not cool water?

FA: I'm sorry. It's my fault. We have run out of cool water, so I was in a hurry to take you some from the thermos. I'm really very sorry. _____.

PX: Well, don't mind, not that serious.

FA: Thank you, sir. Thank you _____.

*任务四　疫情广播

任务导入

本任务收集了四种疫情期间的特殊广播，供大家学习比较。

广播要求

语速中等、咬字清晰；语气委婉诚恳、关切。所有乘客需完成国内、国际航班《健康申明卡》的填写，登机时，乘务员给每位乘客发放纸质版《健康申明卡》并做广播。航班中根据相应标准及程序做好防疫服务、专项信息记录等工作。相关乘客信息需单独回收。

任务要求

通过本任务的学习，学习者应牢记疫情航班高频词汇和句型并能灵活运用；了解疫情期间航班广播和服务的主要程序。

一、疫情广播词

1. 机上测体温

女士们、先生们：

为做好卫生防疫工作，所有抵达＿＿＿＿＿＿＿的航班，乘客需要在机上完成体温检测。现在乘务员将开始进行测温，请您尽快入座，不要更换座位。感谢您的配合。

Taking Temperature

Ladies and gentlemen,

For epidemic prevention, all arriving passengers should complete the temperature checking onboard. Cabin crew will take your temperature right now, please take your seat. Don't change your seat.

Your cooperation will be much appreciated.

2. 平飞广播

女士们、先生们：

飞机已到达巡航高度，为了防止意外颠簸造成伤害，请您务必全程系好安全带。为了做好机上防疫，保障全体乘客的健康安全，本次航班将提供一次性餐具和服务用品，调整餐食饮料，最大程度减少交叉感染。同时，飞机上的空气平均每2至3分钟就会全部更新并排出客舱，请大家不必担心客舱内的空气质量问题。

感谢您的理解与配合。

After Take-off

Ladies and gentlemen,

We have reached the cruising altitude. To prevent injury from turbulence, please keep your seat-belt fastened during the entire flight. To protect your and others' health, we will provide service with disposable tableware and service supply. Meanwhile the meal and beverage selection could be limited. The cabin air circulates every two to three minutes and is expelled from the cabin. Please don't worry about the air quality in the cabin.

Thank you for your understanding.

3. 健康申明卡（所有国际入境航班，见图 4-4 和图 4-5）

女士们、先生们：

根据《中华人民共和国国境卫生检疫法》的要求，为做好防疫工作，所有入境中国的乘客，需要在机上完成乘客申明工作。现在乘务员将为您发放《中华人民共和国出／入境健康申明卡》，每位乘客都必须如实填写，父母或监护人可为子女代填表格。您的个人信息仅用于防控疫情传播，请在下机后将申明卡提交给海关官员，并配合海关做好卫生检疫工作。

谢谢您的合作。

Health Declaration Form

Ladies and gentlemen,

Actions have been put in place by public health authorities at the airport in response to the ongoing outbreak of the Pneumonia Cases caused by Corona virus. Public health authorities require that all travelers complete a health declaration form before arrival. Your information

图 4-4

图 4-5

will be used in accordance with local privacy laws to help fight the spread of the disease. Every traveler must complete a form. A parent or guardian may complete the form for a child. This is required as a precautionary measure even if you are feeling well. The cabin crew will distribute the form shortly. Please hand the completed form to the public health authority representative on arrival.

Thank you for your cooperation.

4. 健康申明卡填写告知（国内抵沪航线）

女士们、先生们：

根据疫情防控工作的需要，所有抵达_____的乘客，须扫描《健康申明卡》上的二维码，完成线上自助填写。

感谢您为防控疫情所做的配合！

Guidance

Ladies and gentlemen,

In order to prevent and control the epidemic situation, all the passengers arrive in _____, please scan the QR code on the card and complete the online filling of health declaration.

Thank you for your cooperation.

词汇

epidemic /ˌepɪˈdemɪk/	adj. 流行的；传染性的
	n. 传染病；流行病
take one's temperature	测体温
cruising altitude	巡航高度
injury /ˈɪndʒəri/	n. 伤害，损害；受伤处
disposable /dɪˈspəʊzəbl/	adj. 可任意处理的；可自由使用的；用完即可丢弃的
tableware /ˈteɪblweə(r)/	n. 餐具
circulate /ˈsɜːkjəleɪt/	vi. 传播，流传；循环；流通
	vt. 使循环；使流通；使传播
expel from	驱逐出；开除；排出
public health authority	公共卫生部门

outbreak /ˈaʊtbreɪk/	n. (战争的)爆发;(疾病的)发作
	vi. 爆发
Pneumonia /njuːˈməʊniə/	n. 肺炎
Corona virus	冠状病毒
in accordance with	依照;与……一致
guardian /ˈɡɑːdiən/	n. 监护人,保护人;守护者
	adj. 守护的
precautionary /prɪˈkɔːʃənəri/	adj. 预防的
QR code	二维码

二、疫情航班情景用语

1. 预防措施

(1) How to prevent virus infection?
应怎样预防病毒感染?

(2) Avoid visiting outbreak areas.
避免去疫情高发区。

(3) Minimize outdoor activities, and wear a face mask when you need to go outdoors.
尽量少出门,需要外出时应佩戴口罩。

(4) Maintain good ventilation indoors.
加强房间开窗通风。

(5) Wash hands frequently and maintain good personal hygiene.
勤洗手,注意个人卫生。

2. 交通记录

(1) What should I do if I recently came to _____ from other regions?
如果近期我从外地到_____该怎么做?

(2) If you came from _____ (疫情地区/城市) or made a transit in _____, please make a note of the time and detailed information (license plate, train or flight number and tickets, seat number, etc.) of the transportation you took.
如果您是从_____而来或是在_____中转,请将您乘坐的交通工具的时间及详细信息(如汽车牌照、火车车次、飞机航班以及座次等)记录下来。

3. 隔离措施

You shall inform the work station of your community, your employer or the hotel you are staying in upon arrival. You are required to undergo a 14-day self-monitored or collective quarantine. Your cooperation with the community staffs, doctors and police officers is highly appreciated.

请在抵达之日主动向所在社区工作站、工作单位或者入住的酒店等申报，您需要居家隔离14天或者集中隔离观察。非常感谢您配合社区工作站工作人员、医生和社区民警的疫情防控管理和服务工作。

词汇

infection /ɪnˈfekʃn/	n. 感染；传染；影响；传染病
outbreak area	暴发地区
minimize /ˈmɪnɪmaɪz/	vt. 使减到最少；小看，极度轻视
	vi. 最小化
go outdoors	去户外；外出
ventilation /ˌventɪˈleɪʃn/	n. 通风设备；空气流通
frequently /ˈfriːkwəntli/	adv. 频繁地，经常地；时常，屡次
hygiene /ˈhaɪdʒiːn/	n. 卫生；卫生学
community /kəˈmjuːnəti/	n. 社区
employer /ɪmˈplɔɪə(r)/	n. 雇主，老板
undergo /ˌʌndəˈɡəʊ/	vt. 经历，经受；忍受

句型

（1）Meanwhile the meal and beverage selection could be limited.
同时，餐食和饮料供应将受限。

（2）In response to the ongoing outbreak of the Pneumonia Cases…
为了应对持续暴发的肺炎病例……

（3）Even if you are feeling well, …
即便您感觉良好（健康），……

（4）Your cooperation with the community staffs, doctors and police officers...

您（的）对社区工作人员、医生、警察（工作）的配合……

（5）Undergo a 14-day self-monitored or collective quarantine.

实施为期 14 天的自我（居家）监控（隔离）或集中隔离。

知识拓展：填写健康申明卡

某航班，一位行动不便的老年乘客需要填写《健康申明卡》，但此女士的手机没有开通网络，需要填写纸质单据。

案例分析

乘务员得知乘客眼睛视力不好，不方便写字时，应及时协助其填写了单据。虽然疫情期间服务流程简化，但作为客舱的主人翁，乘务员要保持着积极温暖的心态，热情有礼，主动与乘客互动，让乘客感受到家的感觉。

任务实践

（1）熟读四段广播词，进行客舱广播实练。

（2）在所给词汇后填写对应的中文或英文。

巡航高度＿＿＿＿＿＿＿＿＿　　take one's temperature ＿＿＿＿＿＿

健康申明卡＿＿＿＿＿＿＿＿　　disposable tableware ＿＿＿＿＿＿

在线填写＿＿＿＿＿＿＿＿＿　　every two to three minutes ＿＿＿＿＿＿

病毒感染＿＿＿＿＿＿＿＿＿　　in response to ＿＿＿＿＿＿

个人卫生＿＿＿＿＿＿＿＿＿　　scan the QR code ＿＿＿＿＿＿

（3）单项选择题。

① My boyfriend comes to see me ＿＿＿＿ weeks.

    A. for two or three   B. every two or three

    C. each two or three   D. on two or three

② In your daily life, we suggest that you do not use ＿＿＿＿ supply.

    A. once   B. reusable   C. plastic   D. disposable

③ ＿＿＿＿ prevent and control the epidemic situation, all arriving passengers should complete health declaration form.

    A. To   B. So as to   C. In order to   D. All of the above

④ You can use your phone to _____ the QR code on the card to pay for it.
　　A. sweep　　　　B. scan　　　　C. clean　　　　D. photo

⑤ When you are in public place, you'd better _____ your phone volume.
　　A. minimize　　B. maximize　　C. adopt　　　　D. silent

（4）句子翻译。

① 请在抵达之日主动向所在社区工作站、工作单位或者入住的酒店等进行申报。
_____

② 应怎样预防新型冠状病毒感染？
_____

③ 您的个人信息仅用于防控疫情传播。
_____

④ 请扫描《健康申明卡》上的二维码，完成线上自助填写。
_____

⑤ 尽量少出门，必须外出时应佩戴口罩。
_____

⑥ To protect your and others' health, we will provide service with disposable tableware and service supply.
_____

⑦ The cabin air circulates every two to three minutes and is expelled from the cabin.
_____

⑧ Please make a note of the time and detailed information of the transportation you took.
_____

⑨ You are required to undergo a 14-day self-monitored or collective quarantine.
_____

⑩ Your cooperation with the community staffs, doctors and police officers is highly appreciated.
_____

（5）参考课文中的知识拓展用英文填空，并分组完成角色演练。

(Passenger Z is calling for help to filling the health declaration form.)

FA: Excuse me, madam, how can I help you?

PX: I didn't catch what the purser said just now. What to do with phones?

FA: Madam, in response to the ongoing outbreak of the Pneumonia Cases caused by Corona virus, _____.

　　PX: But, I heard of phone.

　　FA: Yes, you should use your phone to _____.

　　PA: But I don't have a smart phone, so what should I do?

　　FA: Don't worry, madam, _____, and I will take them here for you.

　　PX: Thank you very much. But as you can see, I have bad eyesight, would you please help me to fill them?

　　FA: Of course. _____.

本项目教学音频

项目五
应急广播教学

项目目标

知识目标	掌握失火广播的英语生词和句型； 掌握释压广播的英语生词和句型； 掌握紧急撤离广播的英语生词和句型； 掌握安全设备示范广播的英语生词和句型。
技能目标	流利地进行失火广播及情景对话； 流利地进行释压广播及情景对话； 流利地进行紧急撤离广播及情景对话； 流利地进行安全设备示范广播及情景对话。
职业素养目标	培养学生爱岗敬业的精神； 培养学生机上广播职业素养； 培养学生对旅客的主动服务意识； 培养学生航班应急处置能力。

任务一　失　火　广　播

任务导入

本项目我们进入应急广播的教学，本项目内容均可与民航乘务专业应急课程结合教学，本任务从客舱失火广播开始，摘选了发现火情、灭火后及客舱发现烟雾（火情前兆）的广播供参考。

广播要求

语速中等偏快、节奏明快、层次清楚；语气坚定、沉稳、自信，不能表现出紧张，并注意正确指导乘客。

> **任务要求**
>
> 通过本任务的学习，学习者应牢记灭火高频词汇和句型并能灵活运用；理解灭火案例，结合应急课程理论学习掌握灭火知识。

一、失火广播词

1. 客舱失火

女士们、先生们：

现在客舱（尾部／前部／中部）有一处失火，请大家不要惊慌，我们正在组织灭火，请您坐好，系好安全带，不要来回走动，火源附近的乘客请听从乘务员的指挥调整您的座位。

谢谢！

On Fire

Ladies and gentlemen,

A minor fire has broken out in the (rear/front/middle) of the cabin. Please don't be panic. We are now putting it out. Passengers sitting near the fire, please change your seats according to the instructions of flight attendants. Please do not leave your seats, and fasten your seat-belts.

Thank you!

2. 灭火后

女士们、先生们：

现在客舱（前部／中部／尾部）的火势已被控制，飞机处于良好状态，我们预计在____点____分到达_____机场。机组全体人员对于给大家带来的不便表示真诚的歉意，并对您所给予的协助表示衷心的感谢。

谢谢！

After Fire

Ladies and gentlemen,

The fire has been completely put out. The plane is cruising, we will arrive at _____ airport on schedule. The arrival time is _____. We are sorry to have disturbed you.

Thank you for your cooperation.

3. 客舱有烟雾

女士们、先生们：

由于客舱（前部／中部／尾部）失火有烟雾，请大家立即弯下腰，低下头，用手帕、衣物等捂住口鼻，请系好安全带。

谢谢！

Smoke

Ladies and gentlemen,

There are a lot of smoke because of a minor fire in the (rear/front/middle) of the cabin. Please bend over and cover your mouth and nose with handkerchief or clothes. Please fasten your seat-belt.

Thank you!

词汇

minor /ˈmaɪnə(r)/	adj. 次要的；较小的
put out	扑灭
completely /kəmˈpliːtli/	adv. 完全地，彻底地；完整地
cruise /kruːz/	vi. 乘船游览；以平稳的速度行驶；巡航
	n. 乘船游览；巡航，巡游
on schedule	按时；按照预定时间
bend over	俯身
clothes /kləʊðz/	n. 衣服

二、客舱失火情景用语

1. 发现火源

（1）I just smelled the smell of burning. What's wrong?

我刚刚闻到有烧焦的味道。发生什么事了？

（2）I am scared about it.

好可怕。

（3）A minor fire has just occurred in the rear galley.

厨房的后面起小火了。

2. 灭火

（1）Get the extinguisher.

拿灭火器来。

（2）All of my colleagues are experienced. The fire has been extinguished.

我的同事们经验丰富，火终于被扑灭了。

（3）Just take it easy. It is under control.

别担心，已经完全控制住了。

3. 灭火后

（1）Is there anyone in the lavatory?

洗手间有人吗？

（2）Please get out immediately.

请马上出来。

（3）Please tell me whether or not you have smoked in the lavatory.

请告诉我您是否在卫生间抽烟了。

（4）None of passengers are allowed to smoke on board, including in the lavatory.

任何人都不允许在飞机上抽烟，包括卫生间。

词汇

smell /smel/	n. 气味，嗅觉；臭味
	v. 嗅，闻；有……气味；察觉到；发出……的气味
scared /skeəd/	adj. 害怕的
galley /ˈgæli/	n. 厨房（专指轮船／飞机上的）
extinguisher /ɪkˈstɪŋgwɪʃə(r)/	n. 灭火器；消灭者
under control	处于控制之下；情况正常
immediately /ɪˈmiːdiətli/	adv. 立即，立刻；直接地
whether /ˈweðə(r)/	conj. 是否；不论

句型

（1）We are sorry to have disturbed you.

很抱歉打扰到您了。

（2）Cover your nose and mouth with handkerchief or clothes.

请用手帕或衣物捂住口鼻。

（3）What's wrong?

怎么了？（发生什么事了？有什么不对吗？）

（4）...whether or not you have smoked in the lavatory.

……您是否（有没有）在卫生间内抽烟了。

知识拓展：发动机着火

某航班，飞机在起飞过程中于跑道上滑行时，一个发动机突然起火燃烧。机场事故救援队伍迅速开始疏散机上乘客，而后飞机油箱发生爆炸。爆炸引起的大火在半个多小时后被扑灭（见图 5-1）。

图 5-1

案例分析

如果飞机在起飞或者着陆时发生火灾，扑救起来还相对容易一些，因为这时可以借助机场专职消防队的力量将火扑灭。但如果飞机在飞行过程中着火，而机组人员又没能及时在火灾发生初期将火扑灭，那么火势就会迅速蔓延，直至失去控制。所以，乘务员在起飞和下降过程中，闻到可疑的气味一定要报告驾驶舱，同时注意稳定周围乘客情绪，不要让乘客随意走动影响飞机配平。情势需要的话，乘务员应相互配合灭火和调整乘客座位及控制客舱，并做好全程的广播。

任务实践

（1）熟读四段广播词，进行客舱广播实练。

（2）在所给词汇后填写对应的中文或英文。

烧焦的味道＿＿＿＿＿＿＿＿＿　　put out ＿＿＿＿＿＿＿＿＿

巡航＿＿＿＿＿＿＿＿＿　　on schedule ＿＿＿＿＿＿＿＿＿

小火＿＿＿＿＿＿＿＿＿　　bend over ＿＿＿＿＿＿＿＿＿

到达时间＿＿＿＿＿＿＿＿＿　　under control ＿＿＿＿＿＿＿＿＿

灭火器＿＿＿＿＿＿＿＿＿　　whether or not ＿＿＿＿＿＿＿＿＿

（3）单项选择题。

① We are sorry to inform you that we cannot arrive the destination ＿＿＿＿＿.

A. as schedule　　　　　　　B. at schedule

C. on schedule　　　　　　　D. in schedule

② I just smelled the smell of burning. ＿＿＿＿＿?

A. What's wrong　　　　　　B. What's up

C. What's the matter　　　　　D. All of the above

③ A minor fire has just ＿＿＿＿＿ in the rear galley, don't worry.

A. occurred　　　　　　　　B. on

C. happening　　　　　　　　D. put out

④ Passengers near the fire, change your seats ＿＿＿＿＿ the instructions.

A. following　　　　　　　　B. according to

C. with　　　　　　　　　　D. under

⑤ The fire has been put out. We are sorry ＿＿＿＿＿ you.

A. to have disturbed　　　　　B. to disturb

C. deprive　　　　　　　　　D. be deprived

（4）句子翻译。

① 现在客舱后部的火势已被控制，飞机处于良好状态。

＿＿＿＿＿＿＿＿＿＿＿＿＿＿＿＿＿＿＿＿＿＿＿＿＿＿＿＿＿＿＿＿＿

② 请告诉我您是否在卫生间吸烟了。

＿＿＿＿＿＿＿＿＿＿＿＿＿＿＿＿＿＿＿＿＿＿＿＿＿＿＿＿＿＿＿＿＿

③ Please bend over and cover your mouth and nose with handkerchief or clothes.

＿＿＿＿＿＿＿＿＿＿＿＿＿＿＿＿＿＿＿＿＿＿＿＿＿＿＿＿＿＿＿＿＿

④ None of passengers are allowed to smoke on board, including in the lavatory.

⑤ Don't worry, all of my colleagues are experienced, please be confident in us.

（5）结合客舱应急处置课程对本任务知识拓展案例进行中英文演练。

任务二　释压广播

任务导入

本任务摘选释压、到达安全高度、释压后紧急下降三篇广播词，供大家结合应急课程学习。

广播要求

语速中等偏快、节奏明快、层次清楚；语气坚定、沉稳、自信，不能表现出紧张，并注意正确指导乘客。

任务要求

通过本任务的学习，学习者应牢记客舱释压高频词汇和句型并能够灵活运用；理解释压案例，结合应急课程理论学习掌握灭火知识。

一、释压广播词

1. 客舱释压及氧气面罩的使用

女士们、先生们：

现在飞机客舱释压，正在紧急下降，请不要惊慌，系紧安全带，氧气面罩自动脱落后，请您用力拉下氧气面罩，将面罩罩在口鼻处，进行正常呼吸，请不要走动。

谢谢！

Cabin Depressurization

Ladies and gentlemen,

This is emergency descending due to the cabin depressurization. Please keep calm. Please fasten your seat-belt and remain in your seats. The oxygen mask will automatically drop from the unit above the seat. When you see the mask, reach up and pull the mask down to your face, cover your nose and mouth, and slip the elastic band over your head. Oxygen will automatically be supplied.

Thank you!

2. 失密后，到达安全高度

女士们、先生们：

现在飞机已到达安全高度，处于正常状态，您可以取下氧气面罩。需要帮助的乘客，请按呼唤铃。

谢谢！

Reaching Safety Altitude

Ladies and gentlemen,

The plane is on the safety altitude and the plane is in a normal situation now. Please take off the oxygen mask. If you need help, please press the call button.

Thank you!

3. 紧急下降

女士们、先生们：

现在飞机紧急下降，请各位乘客系紧安全带、收起小桌板和调直座椅靠背，紧急下降期间请不要离开自己的座位。

谢谢！

Emergency Descending

Ladies and gentlemen,

This is emergency descending. Please fasten your seat-belt, retract your tables and return the seat-backs to the upright position. Please do not leave your seats.

Thank you!

词汇

descend /dɪˈsend/	vi. 下降；下去；下来
	vt. 下去；沿……向下
depressurization /diːˌpreʃəraɪˈzeɪʃn/	n. 降压；减压
cabin depressurization	客舱释压
automatically /ˌɔːtəˈmætɪkli/	adv. 自动地；机械地；无意识地
drop /drɒp/	v. 推动；下降
reach up	抬起（手、足等）
slip /slɪp/	vi. 滑动；滑倒
	vt. 使滑动；滑过；塞入
elastic /ɪˈlæstɪk/	adj. 有弹性的；灵活的；易伸缩的
	n. 松紧带；橡皮圈
oxygen /ˈɒksɪdʒən/	n. 氧气，氧
call button	呼唤铃
retract /rɪˈtrækt/	vt. & vi. 缩回；缩进

二、客舱释压情景用语

（1）I feel stuffy in my chest.
我感觉胸闷。

（2）Maybe, it's caused by cabin depressurization.
可能是客舱释压的原因。

（3）What's the "cabin depressurization"?
什么是"客舱释压"？

（4）In short, it's lack of oxygen.
简单地说，就是缺氧。

（5）Please pull down the oxygen mask and cover your nose and mouth, like this.
请您拉下氧气面罩，戴在口鼻处，就像这样。

（6）Don't panic, just breathe normally.
不要慌，只要正常呼吸就行。

（7）The safety altitude refers to the altitude of 3000 meters or below. In this altitude, passengers aren't deprived of oxygen, so it's called "safety altitude".

安全高度是指海拔 3000 米或以下。这个高度，乘客不会缺氧，因此称为"安全高度"。

（8）We need to divert to a nearby airport for making inspection and maintenance. Safety is our top priority.

我们需要转向附近机场对飞机进行检修。安全是最重要的。

词汇

stuffy /ˈstʌfi/	*adj.* 闷热的；古板的；不通气的
lack of	没有；不够；缺乏，不足
pull down	推翻；拉下来
panic /ˈpænɪk/	*n.* 恐慌，惊慌；大恐慌
	adj. 恐慌的；没有理由的
	vt. 使恐慌
	vi. 十分惊慌
breathe /briːð/	*vi.* 呼吸；低语；（风）轻拂
	vt. 呼吸；使喘息
be deprived /dɪˈpraɪvd/ of	被剥夺，被夺去
divert /daɪˈvɜːt/	*vt.* 转移；使……转向
	vi. 转移
inspection /ɪnˈspekʃn/	*n.* 视察，检查
maintenance /ˈmeɪntənəns/	*n.* 维护，维修；保持
priority /praɪˈɒrəti/	*n.* 优先；优先权；优先考虑的事

句型

（1）The plane is on the safety altitude.

飞机处于安全高度。

（2）The plane is in a normal situation.

飞机处于正常状态。

（3）The safety altitude refers to the altitude of 3000 meters or below.

安全高度是指海拔 3000 米及以下。

（4）In short, it's lack of oxygen.

简而言之（简单地说），就是缺氧。

知识拓展：客舱释压

某航班由于机组没有做好安全检查和释压正确的处置方式，乘务员被吸起来，副驾被吸出窗外。

案例分析

客舱释压（见图 5-2）时，无论乘务员还是乘客，第一时间都要系好安全带固定好自己，再拉下氧气面罩吸氧。释压分为快速释压和缓慢释压，快速释压参考本案例的客舱现象，要求乘客拉下氧气面罩吸氧后系安全带是因为释压缺氧容易昏迷。缓慢释压时客舱灯会全亮，释压广播响起，乘客只要听指令拉氧气面罩吸氧就好，卫生间里也有面罩，旁边有扶手，一定要固定好自己，听从广播和乘务员的指挥，先大人后小孩，因为释压在高空缺氧有知觉时间很短，可能在给小孩子戴的时候已经昏迷。另外，平时飞机遇到颠簸，乘务员即刻广播要求乘客坐好系好安全带也是一种预防释压的措施。

图 5-2

任务实践

（1）熟读三段广播词，进行客舱广播实练。
（2）在所给词汇后填写对应的中文或英文。

客舱释压_____　　emergency descending_____
氧气面罩_____　　elastic band_____
缺氧_____　　in a normal situation_____
保持冷静_____　　upright position_____
自动脱落_____　　call button_____

（3）单项选择题。

① You can _____ the oxygen masks when the cabin is pressurized successfully.

　　A. take off　　　　　　　　　B. put off

　　C. kick off　　　　　　　　　D. get off

② If you want to pick apples, you should _____ your hands _____.

　　A. reach; up　　　　　　　　B. reach; out

　　C. reach; to　　　　　　　　D. reach; for

③ Once your hands are there, the water will _____ flow on them.

　　A. voluntarily　　　　　　　B. automatically

　　C. automatic　　　　　　　　D. selfishly

④ Take it easy, Jack, not you, I _____ the one behind you.

　　A. refer to　　　　　　　　　B. point to

　　C. prefer to　　　　　　　　D. infer to

⑤ The so-called "safety altitude" indicates that passengers will not _____ oxygen.

　　A. deprive of　　　　　　　　B. be deprived of

　　C. deprive　　　　　　　　　D. be deprived

（4）句子翻译。

① 现在飞机客舱释压，正在紧急下降，请不要惊慌，系紧安全带。

_____

② 氧气面罩自动脱落后，请您用力拉下氧气面罩，将面罩罩在口鼻处，正常呼吸。

_____

③ If you need help, please press the call button.

_____

④ Please fasten your seat-belt, retract your tables and return the seat-backs to the upright position.

_____

⑤ We need to divert to a nearby airport for making inspection and maintenance. Safety is our top priority.

_____

（5）结合客舱应急处置课程对本任务知识拓展案例进行中英文演练。

任务三　紧急撤离广播

任务导入

本任务我们学习紧急撤离广播，本任务内容可与民航乘务专业应急课程结合教学，一般我们将民航紧急撤离分为水上迫降和陆地迫降两种，而水上迫降又可分为有准备的水上迫降和有限时间的水上迫降，陆地迫降也可分为有准备的陆地迫降和有限时间的陆地迫降，而本任务选取了有准备陆地迫降的客舱准备广播、有准备陆地迫降选择援助者并更换座位广播、有准备陆地迫降机门口援助者分工广播，其他三种迫降同类型广播可按此变化学习。水上迫降的某些特别广播内容我们将在下个任务和安全设备示范广播一起学习。

广播要求

语速偏快、节奏明快、层次清楚；语气坚定、沉稳、自信，不能表现出紧张，并注意正确指导乘客。第一和第三段都是应急指令广播，所以必须一句中文一句英文，让所有乘客第一时间听清楚指令和要求，最后一段选择援助者广播一般一名乘务员对三名乘客同时说，建议背诵。

任务要求

通过本任务的学习，学习者应牢记紧急迫降高频词汇和句型并能够灵活运用；结合应急课程理论学习掌握紧急撤离知识。

一、紧急撤离广播词

1. 客舱准备
Cabin Ready

女士们、先生们：

请注意，我们已决定采取陆地迫降。请乘客们回座位坐好，保持安静，注意并听从乘务员的指挥。

Ladies and gentlemen,

It is necessary to make an emergency landing. Please return to your seats , keep calm and follow our directions.

（注：此时乘务员应整理厨房，帮助乘客存放行李。）

请将您的餐盘和所有其他服务用具准备好，以便乘务员收取。

Pass your food tray and all other service items for picking up.

调直座椅靠背，固定好小桌板。收起脚踏板和座位上的录像装置。

Bring seat-backs to the upright position and stow all tray tables. Stow footrests and in-seat video units.

（注：此时乘务员在客舱内强调并督促乘客完成以上操作。）

为了撤离时您的安全，请取下随身的尖锐物品，如钢笔、手表和首饰，取下领带和围巾等物品。把所有这些物品放入行李内，请不要把任何东西放在您前面的座椅袋内。

Ladies and gentlemen, please remove sharp objects, such as pens, watches, jewelry to prevent injury. Remove neckties and scarves. Put them in your baggage, do not put anything in the seat-pocket in front of you.

（注：此时暂停广播乘务员在客舱内强调并督促乘客完成以上操作。）

现在，请大家取出衣服穿好，把所有行李放入行李架内。脱下高跟鞋交由乘务员保管。系紧安全带。

Now, everybody take your coats and put them on. Please put all your baggage in the overhead locker. Remove high-heeled shoes and hand them to your flight attendants. Fasten your seat belt tight and low.

（注：此段没说完一句话，暂停一次，乘务员协助乘客完成相关操作并回复广播员完成手势。）

2. 选择援助者

女士们、先生们：

请注意：如果您是航空公司的雇员、执法人员、消防人员或军人的话，请与乘务员联络，我们需要您的协助。同时，根据机长的要求，我们将调整一些人的座位。

Choose and Relocate Helpers

Ladies and gentlemen,

Please contact our flight attendants if you are an employee of airlines, law enforcement personnel, firefighter or military service personnel. We appreciate your assistance. Please cooperate as we relocate passengers according to the instructions from the captain.

3. 机门口援助者分工
Helpers at the Door

请做我的援助者。

Please be my helper.

像这样挡住乘客，直到滑梯完全充气。

Block passengers like this until the slide is fully inflated.

如果我不能开门，请帮我打开。

If I cannot open the door, please help me.

（注：此时乘务员指导援助者开门及滑梯充气方式。）

注意观察机外情况，如有烟雾、起火和障碍物等情况不要开门，指挥乘客去其他出口。

Assess the situation outside, if there is smoke, fire or obstruction, don't open the door, and direct passengers to evacuate through other exits.

你们两个先跳下滑梯，在滑梯两侧帮助乘客撤离并指挥他们远离飞机。

You and you jump the slide first. Help passengers on both sides of the slide and direct them to run away from the plane.

你在门口像我一样抓住这个把手，指挥乘客"快往这边来，跳，滑"。

You hold the door handle like me, and direct passengers, "this way, hurry, jump, slide".

如果我受伤，将我带下飞机，我的安全带是这样解开的。

If I'm injured, please take me away from the plane.

（注：此时乘务员想援助者介绍安全带的解开方式，并请他们重复任务。完成后乘务员帮助援助者更换座位，重复防冲击姿势及确认安全带是否扣紧。）

词汇

calm /kɑːm/	adj. 静的，平静的；沉着的
direction /dəˈrekʃn/	n. 方向；指导
foot tray	脚踏板 / 脚蹬（也可用 footrest）
extinguish /ɪkˈstɪŋgwɪʃ/	vt. 熄灭
cigarette /ˌsɪgəˈret/	n. 香烟；纸烟

unit /ˈjuːnɪt/	n. 单位，单元；装置
jewelry /ˈdʒuːəlrɪ/	n. 珠宝
necktie /ˈnektaɪ/	n. 领带
scarf /skɑːf/	n. 围巾；头巾领巾
high-heeled shoes	高跟鞋（也可用 high-heels）
employee /ɪmˈplɔiː/	n. 雇员；从业员工
enforcement /ɪnˈfɔːsmənt/	n. 执行，实施；强制
firefighter /ˈfaɪəfaɪtə(r)/	n. 消防队员
military /ˈmɪlətri/	adj. 军事的；军人的；适于战争的
	n. 军队；军人
cooperate /kəʊˈɒpəreɪt/	vi. 合作，配合；协力
relocate /ˌriːləʊˈkeɪt/	vt. 重新安置；迁移
	vi. 重新安置；迁移新址
block /blɒk/	vt. 阻止；阻塞；限制；封盖
slide /slaɪd/	n. 滑梯
	v. 滑动
inflate /ɪnˈfleɪt/	vt. 使充气
	vi. 膨胀；充气
assess /əˈses/	vt. 评定；估价
evacuate /ɪˈvækjueɪt/	vt. & vi. 疏散，撤退，撤离
direct /dəˈrekt; daɪˈrekt/	vt. 管理；指挥；指向
	vi. 指导；指挥
handle /ˈhændl/	n.（门的）把手；柄

二、紧急撤离情景用语

1. 陆地迫降准备

（1）Excuse me, sir. Please pass your food tray and all other service items for collection.
　　对不起，先生。请把盘子递给我，并把其他物品放好以备收集。

（2）Can you give me some details about the mechanical difficulties? Is it serious?
　　能给我们讲一下关于机械故障的细节吗？故障严重吗？

（3）Oh, don't worry about it. We will ensure the safety of the passengers. Now please fasten your seat belt, bring your seat back to the upright position and stow all tray tables.

哦，不用担心。我们一定会确保乘客的安全。现在请系好安全带，调直座椅靠背，收起小桌板。

（4）Please, listen! When instructed to brace for impact, put your legs apart, and place your feet flat on the floor.

注意！防止冲撞时，须两腿分开，双脚蹬地。

（5）Thank you for your participation. We will be asking you to change seats to better help those needing assistance or to be closer to an exit to help evacuate.

感谢你们的参与。我们将要求你们调换座位，以帮助那些需要帮助的人，或在紧急出口帮助乘客撤离。

2. 水上迫降准备

（1）Miss, can you show me one more time?

女士，能否再演示一遍？

（2）OK. Your life vest is located under your seat. Find it? ...Pull the tab to open the pouch and remove the life vest. Do you find the tab?

行。您的救生衣在您的座位下方，找到了吗？……把那个标签拉下来，打开包装，找到那个标签了吗？

（3）Wait a moment. Let me review it again... OK, go on.

等一下，让我复习一遍……好了，继续吧。

（4）Now please remain seated and don't touch the vest.

现在请在座位上坐好，不要触碰救生衣。

词汇

collection /kəˈlekʃn/	n. 采集，聚集；征收
serious /ˈsɪəriəs/	adj. 严肃的，严重的；危急的
upright /ˈʌpraɪt/	adj. 垂直的，直立的；笔直的
	n. 垂直；竖立
brace /breɪs/	v. 抵住；绷紧；支撑
impact /ˈɪmpækt/	n. 碰撞；冲击力
flat /flæt/	adv.（尤指贴着另一表面）平直地；水平地

tab /tæb/	n. 标签
pouch /paʊtʃ/	n. 小袋
life vest/vest/	救生衣（也可用 vest）
remove /rɪˈmuːv/	vt. & vi. 移动，迁移
review /rɪˈvjuː/	n. 回顾；复习
	vt. 回顾；检查；复审
	vi. 回顾
remain /rɪˈmeɪn/	vi. 保持

句型

（1）It is necessary to...
必须要（做）……

（2）Please remove sharp objects, such as pens, watches...
请取下尖锐物品，比如钢笔，手表……

（3）direct passengers to evacuate through other exits.
带领乘客从其他出口撤离。

（4）Your life vest is located under your seat.
您的救生衣位于座椅下方。

（5）You hold the door handle like me.
像我这样抓住门把手。

知识拓展：紧急出口

某航班飞机下降时，乘务员将自己的箱包和装满物品的塑料袋放在2L门处。落地后，开门时，塑料袋和箱包被机门卡住，机门（见图5-3）因此断电而无法开启，当时满舱的乘客在机上足足等了40分钟，影响极大，以至于被媒体曝光。

图 5-3

案例分析

《乘务员手册》明文规定："紧急出口处禁止堆放物品。"责任乘务员无视规定，带班乘务长对飞机下降时段的安全检查监督不够，正常情况下不能开门影响乘客下机，紧急情况下影响乘客撤离，少了一扇应急门就少了一条逃生通道。

任务实践

（1）熟读两段广播词和情景用语，进行客舱广播实练。

（2）在所给词汇后填写对应的中文或英文。

紧急撤离＿＿＿＿＿＿＿＿＿＿　　service items ＿＿＿＿＿＿＿＿＿＿

消防队员＿＿＿＿＿＿＿＿＿＿　　brace for impact ＿＿＿＿＿＿＿＿＿＿

军（事服役）人（员）＿＿＿＿＿＿＿＿　　one more time ＿＿＿＿＿＿＿＿＿＿

高跟鞋＿＿＿＿＿＿＿＿＿＿　　life vest ＿＿＿＿＿＿＿＿＿＿

尖锐物品＿＿＿＿＿＿＿＿＿＿　　foot tray ＿＿＿＿＿＿＿＿＿＿

（3）单项选择题。

① Please pass your food tray and all other service items ＿＿＿＿＿＿＿.

　　A. for me to pick up　　　　　　B. for picking up

　　C. for my collection　　　　　　D. All of the above

② You can put ＿＿＿＿＿＿＿ in the seat-pocket in front of you.

　　A. everything　　B. anything　　C. something　　D. nothing

③ Block passengers ＿＿＿＿＿＿＿ this until the slide is fully inflated.

　　A. like　　　　B. unlike　　　　C. dislike　　　　D. likely

④ Help passengers on ＿＿＿＿＿＿＿ of the slide and direct them to run away from the plane.

　　A. both sides　　B. all sides　　C. every side　　D. each side

⑤ In order to evacuate better, we will ＿＿＿＿＿＿＿ the passengers.

　　A. review　　　B. remove　　　C. relocate　　　D. reload

（4）句子翻译。

① 女士们、先生们，我们必须采取紧急迫降。

_____

② 调直座椅靠背，固定好小桌板。收起脚踏板和座位上的录像装置。

_____

③ 如果您是航空公司的雇员、执法人员、消防人员或军人，请与乘务员联络。

_____

④ 你们两位站在滑梯两侧，帮助乘客，并指挥他们远离飞机。

_____

⑤ 请注意观察机外情况，如有烟雾、起火和障碍物等情况，请不要开门，并指挥乘客从其他出口撤离。

_____

⑥ Please pass your food tray and all other service items for collection.

_____

⑦ We are sure to ensure the safety of the passengers onboard.

_____

⑧ When instructed to brace for impact, put your legs apart, and place your feet flat on the floor.

_____

⑨ We will relocate your seats to better help those needing assistance or to be closer to an exit to help evacuate.

_____

⑩ Can you give me some details about the mechanical difficulties? Is it serious?

_____

（5）参考课文中的知识拓展用英文填空，并分组完成角色演练。

(Passenger X cannot put on the life vest properly in water evacuation.)

　　FA: Ladies and gentlemen, it's necessary to _____. Now, please listen to me carefully. The life vest _____.

　　PX: Help, I cannot find the life vest, is there no one for me?

　　FA: Don't worry, madam. We did do the pre-flight preparation.

　　PX: OK, under my own seat. Yes, I got it, a pouch.

　　FA: Good! _____.

　　PA: OK, the tab, open the pouch. So what should I do next?

FA: Put it on, BUT, don't _____ until _____.

PX: OK. I will follow others.

FA: Thank you for your cooperation.

任务四　安全设备示范广播

任务导入

本任务主要学习安全设备示范广播和水上迫降的救生衣检查和寻求翼上援助者广播内容，本任务课程的广播建议与空乘应急课程一起学习。

广播要求

语速偏快、节奏明快、层次清楚；语气坚定、沉稳、自信，不能表现出紧张，并注意正确指导乘客，演示的乘务员每一个动作节拍都不能错。第一和第一段都是应急指令广播，所以必须一句中文一句英文，让所有乘客第一时间听清楚指令和要求，最后一段选择水上迫降的翼上援助者比较难一点，作为学生教学可以选学。

任务要求

通过本任务的学习，学习者应牢记安全演示和紧急迫降设备演示、寻找援助者的高频词汇和句型并能够灵活运用；结合应急课程理论学习掌握安全设备各项示范和广播。

一、安全设备示范广播词

1. 客舱安全设备示范
Safety Demonstration

女士们、先生们：

现在由客舱乘务员向您演示救生衣、氧气面罩、安全带的使用方法和紧急出口的位置。

Ladies and gentlemen,

We will now demonstrate the use of the life vest, oxygen mask, the seat-belt and the location of the exits.

救生衣在您座椅下面。

Your life vest is located under your seat.

使用时取出，经头部穿好。

To put the vest on, slip it over your head.

将带子扣好、系紧。

Fasten the buckles and pull the straps tight around your waist.

然后，打开充气阀门。

Then pull the inflation tab.

但在客舱内请不要充气。（重复）

Please do not inflate it while you are in the cabin.（repeat）

充气不足时，可将救生衣上部的两个人工充气管拉出，用嘴向里充气。

If your vest is not inflated enough, you can inflate it by blowing into the mouth pieces.

氧气面罩储藏在您座椅上方。

The oxygen mask is in the compartment over your head.

发生紧急情况时，面罩会自动脱落。

It will appear automatically when needed.

氧气面罩脱落后，要用力向下拉面罩。

If you see the mask, pull the mask toward you firmly to start the flow of oxygen.

将面罩罩在口鼻处，带子套在头上，进行正常呼吸。

Place the mask over your nose and mouth, slip the elastic band over your head. Within a few seconds, oxygen flow will begin.

带小孩的乘客先戴好您的面罩，然后再帮助您的小孩。

There are also masks for your kids, please put your mask at first, then assist your kids.

这是您座椅上的安全带。

This is the seat-belt on your seat.

将连接片插入锁扣内即固定安全带。

To fasten your seat-belt, insert the link into the main buckle.

根据您的需要，调节安全带的松紧。

To be effective, the seat-belt should be fastened tight and low.

解开时，先将锁扣打开，拉出连接片。

To unfasten the seat-belt, lift the flap and pull out the link.

本架飞机除了正常出口外，在客舱的左右侧还有紧急出口，分别写有紧急出口的明显标志。

There are emergency exits on each side of the aircraft in addition to the main entrance doors. All the exits are clearly marked.

客舱通道及出口处都设有紧急照明灯，紧急情况下请按指示灯路线撤离飞机。

The lights located on the floor will guide you to the exits if an emergency arises.

安全说明书在您座椅前面的口袋里，请您在起飞前仔细阅读。

For further information, please refer to the safety instruction leaflet before take-off.

谢谢！

Thank you!

（注：本段广播属于应急广播中最常用的广播，每次航班如果安全须知录像不能播放，整个乘务组必须在起飞前进行安全设备示范广播和演示。本篇标有"＿＿"的地方都是演示时为了整齐统一动作演示的地方，而全篇有一句标有"＿＿"的句子要重复广播两次。）

➡ 2. 救生衣演示 ⬅
Explain the Use of Life Vest

女生们、先生们：

现在乘务员将向您演示救生衣的使用方法，请从座位下取出救生衣，随同乘务员的演示穿上救生衣，但在客舱内不要充气。

Ladies and gentlemen,

Now we will explain the use of life vest. Please take out your life vest under your seat and follow the demonstration of your flight attendants to put it on. But do not inflate it while you are in the cabin.

撕开包装，将救生衣经头部穿好，将带子扣好，系紧。

To put the vest on, slip it over your head, then fasten the buckles and pull the straps tight around your waist.

当你离开飞机时，拉下救生衣两侧的红色充气把手，但在客舱内不要充气。

Just before leaving the aircraft. Pull the red tabs to inflate your vest, but do not inflate it while you are in the cabin.

充气不足时，可将救生衣上部的人工充气管拉出，用嘴吹气。

If your vest is not inflated enough, you can also inflate it by blowing into the tubes.

（注：此时广播暂停，乘务员迅速划分乘客的撤离区域，演示出口并加以确认。标有"＿＿＿"的句子重复广播两次。）

➡ *3. 翼上窗援助者 ⬅
For Helpers at Over-wing Windows

请做我的援助者。

Please be my helper.

判断机外情况，打开出口（介绍出口操作方式），如果水位过高、门外有火不要开门，指挥乘客去其他出口，命令出口处的乘客救生衣充气，协助我取出救生船，跟随我的指令操作，帮助乘客登船，分散坐下。

(Show helpers the nearest alternate exit.) Tell passengers to inflate vests at the door and help me to take out raft. Follow my instructions to direct passengers to board the raft and spread out to sit.

词汇

demonstrate /ˈdemənstreɪt/	vt. 演示；展示
buckle /ˈbʌkl/	n. 带扣
location /ləʊˈkeɪʃn/	n. 位置；地点
strap /stræp/	n. 带子，皮带
waist /weɪst/	n. 腰，腰部
inflation /ɪnˈfleɪʃn/	n. 充气阀门
blow /bləʊ/	v.（风）吹；喘气；吹气
appear /əˈpɪə(r)/	vi. 出现
automatically /ˌɔːtəˈmætɪkli/	adv. 自动地；机械地
firmly /ˈfɜːmli/	adv. 坚定地；坚固地，稳固地
elastic /ɪˈlæstɪk/	adj. 有弹性的；易伸缩的
flow /fləʊ/	n. 流动；传播；流通
assist /əˈsɪst/	v. 协助（做一部分工作）
insert /ɪnˈsɜːt/	v. 插入；嵌入
effective /ɪˈfektɪv/	adj. 有效的，起作用的
flap /flæp/	n. 锁扣

pull out	拉出，抽出
entrance /ˈentrəns/	n. 入口；进入
guide /ɡaɪd/	vt. 引导；带领
arise /əˈraɪz/	vi. 出现；上升
explain /ɪkˈspleɪn/	vt. 说明；解释
tube /tjuːb/	n. 管
condition /kənˈdɪʃn/	n. 条件；情况；环境
alternate /ɔːlˈtɜːnət/	adj.（一或多个事物）另外的，可供选择的
raft /rɑːft/	n. 筏；救生艇

二、安全设备示范情景用语

（1）Fasten your seat-belts immediately. The plane will make an emergency landing because of the sudden breakdown of an engine.

立刻系好安全带。由于飞机发动机出了毛病将做紧急迫降。

（2）Our captain has full confidence to land safely. All the crew members of this flight are well trained for this kind of situation. So please obey instructions from us.

我们的机长完全有信心安全着陆。我们所有的机组人员在这方面都受过良好的训练，请听从我们的指挥。

（3）The crew are well trained to handle this situation. We will do everything necessary to ensure your safety.

我们全体机组人员都受过良好的训练，有信心、有能力保证你们的安全。

（4）Now let me explain how to use the life vests.

现在让我来介绍一下救生衣的使用方法。

（5）Bend your head between your knees! Bend down and grab your ankles.

把您的头弯下来放在两膝之间，弯下身来，抓住脚踝。

（6）Unfasten seat belts, leave everything behind and come this way!

解开安全带，别拿行李，朝这边走！

（7）This plane has eight emergency exits. Please locate the exit nearest to you.

本架飞机有八个安全门，请找到离您最近的那个门。

（8）Now please take this position, so that the flight attendants can assist you.

请大家保持这种姿势，以便乘务员检查。

词汇

immediately /ɪˈmiːdiətli/	adv. 立即，立刻；直接地
	conj. 一……就
sudden /ˈsʌdn/	adj. 突然的，意外的
breakdown /ˈbreɪkdaʊn/	n. 故障；崩溃
engine /ˈendʒɪn/	n. 引擎，发动机
confidence /ˈkɒnfɪdəns/	n. 信心；信任
situation /ˌsɪtʃuˈeɪʃn/	n. 情况；形势；处境；位置
obey /əˈbeɪ/	vt. 服从，听从；按照……行动
	vi. 服从，顺从
necessary /ˈnesəsəri/	adj. 必要的；必需的
grab /græb/	vt. 攫取
	vi. 攫取；夺取
	n. 攫取；霸占
ankle /ˈæŋkl/	n. 踝关节，踝
position /pəˈzɪʃn/	n. 位置，方位；姿态；站位

句型

（1）Please do not inflate it while you are in the cabin.
当您还在客舱内的时候，请不要充气。

（2）You can inflate it by blowing into the mouth pieces.
您可以通过向吹气口吹气的方式对其充气。

（3）It will appear automatically when needed.
需要的时候，它会自动出现。

（4）There are emergency exits on each side of the aircraft in addition to the main entrance doors.
除主登机口以外，机身两侧都有紧急出口。

（5）For further information, please refer to the safety instruction leaflet before take-off.
（若要获得）更多信息，请在起飞前参照安全说明书。

知识拓展：机门滑梯误操作

某航班，乘务员进行安全检查时，突然听到"嘭"的一声，原来3L紧急出口门被好奇的乘客打开，所幸滑梯未充气。虽然地面机务及时进行了处理，但造成了航班的延误。

案例分析

当出口座位乘客入座后，责任乘务员应立即进行出口座位的乘客评估，介绍其出口座位说明书，并做必要的说明和判断确认。地面放映《安全须知》时，外场乘务员应在客舱内与乘客一起观看，观察乘客动向，并针对乘客的需求提供一些必要的服务，这同时也是为紧急情况做准备。

任 务 实 践

（1）熟读三篇演示广播词，进行客舱广播实练。

（2）在所给词汇后填写对应的中文或英文。

氧气面罩_____　　safety demonstration _____

充气阀门_____　　mouth pieces _____

橡皮筋（带）_____　　emergency exits _____

水平面（水位）_____　　over-wing windows _____

分散就座_____　　safety instruction leaflet _____

（3）单项选择题。

① To put the vest on, slip it _____ your head.

　　A. over　　　　B. across　　　　C. through　　　　D. past

② Please do not inflate it while you are in the cabin. Which of the followings can replace the underlined "while"?

　　A. but　　　　B. although　　　　C. when　　　　D. meanwhile

③ If your car is stuck in muddy road, you can ask for help _____ the police.

　　A. to call　　　B. by calling　　　C. by call on　　　D. with calling

④ _____, I will borrow that book for reference.

　　A. If necessary　B. If it necessary　C. If unnecessary　D. If it is unnecessary

⑤ What should I do if an emergency _____? Which of the followings is NOT the answer?

　　A. arises　　　B. comes up　　　C. rises　　　D. breaks down

（4）句子翻译。

① 发生紧急情况时，面罩会自动脱落。

② 将面罩罩在口鼻处，带子套在头上，进行正常呼吸。

③ 充气不足时，可将救生衣上部的两个人工充气管拉出，用嘴向里充气。

④ 带小孩的乘客先戴好您的面罩，然后再帮助您的小孩。

⑤ 判断机外情况，打开出口，如果水位过高、门外有火不要开门。

⑥ The lights located on the floor will guide you to the exits if an emergency arises.

⑦ There are emergency exits on each side of the aircraft in addition to the main entrance doors. All the exits are clearly marked.

⑧ We will now demonstrate the use of the life vest, oxygen mask, the seat-belt and the location of the exits.

⑨ Follow my instructions to direct passengers to board the raft and spread out to sit.

⑩ Please take out your life vest under your seat and follow the demonstration of your flight attendants to put it on.

（5）根据图 5-4 所给的中文说明结合图片动作流利地用英文对新版防冲击姿势进行说明。

当您听到防冲击指令时：
请将下巴紧贴胸部，
向前弯曲，
把头抵在前面的座椅背上，
双手抱住小腿；
如果您前面没有座椅或不能触及前方座椅的靠背，
请向前弯曲，
双手放在头顶。

前排旅客座椅的防冲击姿势
仅配备带式安全带

本项目教学音频

图 5-4

附 录

附录一 机上餐食、酒类中英文名称对照表

中 文	英 文	中 文	英 文
西红柿汁	tomato juice	苏格兰威士忌	Scotch whisky
雪梨汁	pear juice	金酒	Gin
橙汁	orange juice	伏特加	Vodka
芒果汁	mango juice	香槟	Champagne
桃汁	peach juice	起泡酒	sparkling wine
椰子汁	coconut juice	白葡萄酒	white wine
菠萝汁	pineapple juice	红葡萄酒	red wine
葡萄汁	grape juice	啤酒	beer
猕猴桃汁	kiwi juice	柠檬茶	lemon tea
苹果汁	apple juice	绿茶	green tea
低糖可乐	diet coca	红茶	black tea
可口可乐	Coca Cola	茉莉花茶	jasmine tea
七喜	Seven up	洋甘菊茶	Chamomile tea
雪碧	Sprite	奶茶	milk tea
矿泉水	mineral water	普洱茶	Pu'er tea
依云水	Evian	乌龙茶	oolong tea
巴黎水	Perrier	法式长棍	baguette
青柠汁	lime juice	吐司	toast
干姜汁	ginger ale	意大利扁平长面包	ciabatta
甘柠汽水	bitter lemon	香草包	focaccia
汤力水	tonic water	法式牛角包	croissant

中文	英文	中文	英文
苏打水	soda (water)	松饼	muffin
白兰地	Brandy	长条面包	loaf
干邑	Cognac	卷、小面包	roll
威士忌	Whisky	黑麦面包	rye roll
全麦面包	whole wheat roll	大虾（仁）	king prawns
蒜蓉面包	garlic bread	龙虾	lobster
甜甜圈	donut	早餐	breakfast（缩写 BRF）
鱼子酱	caviar	午餐	lunch（缩写"LCH"）
鹅肝酱	goose liver paste	晚餐、正餐	dinner（缩写"DNR"）
生熏鲑鱼片	smoked salmon	快餐	snack（缩写"SNX"）
生熏火腿	smoked ham	点心	refreshment（缩写"REF"）
芝士	cheese	素食	vegetarian meal（缩写"VGML"）
车达	cheddar	糖尿病餐	diabetes meal（缩写"DBML"）
红波	edam	婴儿餐	baby meal（缩写"BBML"）
金文笔	camembert	印度餐	Hindu meal（缩写"HNML"）
丹麦蓝	Danish blue	鲜水果餐	fruit platter meal（缩写"FPML"）
色拉	salad	溃疡餐	bland meal（缩写"BLML"）
汤	soup	犹太餐	Kosher meal（缩写"KSML"）
烤鸡胸	baked chicken breast	儿童餐	child meal（缩写"CHML"）
烤鸡	roast chicken	穆斯林餐	Moslem meal（缩写"MOML"）
烩牛肉	stewed beef	低卡路里餐	low calorie meal（缩写"LCML"）
肉眼牛排	rib-eye steak	低苏打含量，无盐餐	low salt meal（缩写"LSML"）
烤牛肉	roast beef	流食	Liquid(diet)（缩写"LIET"）
牛排	beef steak	低胆固醇，低脂肪餐	low fat meal（缩写"LFML"）
烧烤排骨	barbecued spare ribs	海鲜餐	seafood meal（缩写"SFML"）
炸猪排	fried pork chop	生蔬菜餐	vegetarian raw meal（缩写"RVML"）
扒羊排	grilled lamb chop	无乳糖餐	non-lactose meal（缩写"NLML"）
海鲜	seafood	东方素餐	vegetarian oriental meal（缩写"VOML"）
三文鱼	tuna	无麸（fū）质餐	gluten intolerant meal（缩写"GFML"）
鱼柳	fish fillet		

*附录二 机上急救医疗中英文对照表

中文全称	英文全称	中文全称	英文全称
疼痛	ache	心脏病发作	heart attack
心绞痛；咽喉痛	angina	中暑	heat stroke
中风	apoplexy	幻觉	illusion
心律失常	arrhythmia	流行性感冒	influenza (Flu)
动脉硬化	arteriosclerosis	分娩阵痛	labour pain
哮喘	asthma	腰痛	low back pain
短暂昏厥	black out	流鼻血	nasal bleeding
支气管炎	bronchitis	流鼻涕	nasal discharge
骨折	bone fracture	恶心	nausea
脑栓塞	cerebral embolism	麻痹	numb
发冷	chills	中耳炎	otitis media
被鱼刺噎住了	be choked by a fishbone	中毒	poisoning
流冷汗	cold sweating	怀孕	pregnant
（尤指婴儿的）急性腹痛；腹绞痛	colic	瞳孔放大	pupil dilation
昏迷	coma	皮疹	rash
感冒	(common) cold	烫伤	scald
脑震荡	concussion	喷嚏	sneeze
耳鸣	ear ring	痰	sputum
耳痛	earache	鼻塞	nasal obstruction
癫痫	epilepsy	眩晕	vertigo
昏厥	faint	昏迷	unconsciousness
胎动	fetal movement	呕吐	vomit
发烧	fever	上呼吸道感染	upper respiratory infection
胃溃疡	gastric ulcer	气管炎	tracheitis
胃炎	gastritis	耳鸣	tinnitus
腹痛	general abdominal pain	牙痛	toothache
头痛	headache	分娩	childbearing

*附录三　机上应急处置中英文对照表

中文名称	英文名称
生存组件（SK包）	survival kit
救生衣	life vest
安全演示包	security demo package
手提氧气瓶	portable oxygen bottle
带有防烟面罩的手提氧气瓶	portable oxygen bottle with smoke mask attached
人工释放工具	manual release tool
加长安全带	extension seat belt
防烟面罩	smoke hood
海伦灭火瓶	fire extinguisher (Halon)
救生斧	crash axe
急救药箱	first aid kit
自动体外除颤仪	AED (automated external defibrillator)
紧急定位发报机	ELT (emergency locator transmitter)
应急手电筒	emergency flashlight
二氧化碳灭火瓶	carbon dioxide (CO_2) fire extinguisher
水灭火瓶	fire extinguisher (water)
喇叭/扩音器	megaphone
防护手套（石棉手套）	protective gloves
逃离绳	escape rope
危险品处置包	dangerous goods
防烟护目镜	smoke goggles
带有逃生绳的出口通道	exit path with escape strap
带有撤离滑梯的出口通道	exit path with escape slide
没有撤离滑梯的出口通道	exit path without escape strap
救生筏	life raft
创可贴	band-aid
胶布	adhesive tape
氨吸入剂	ammonia inhalants
消毒棉签	antiseptic swab
自动灭火装置	automatic fire extinguisher
舀水袋	bailing bucket
绷带	bandage
绷带贴	bandage compress
信标/灯塔	beacon attachment

续表

中文名称	英文名称
登筏处	boarding stirrup
烧伤药膏	burn cream/ burn ointment
帐篷与支撑杆	canopy and support mast
帐篷支撑柱	canopy support tube
应急净化饮用水	emergency purified drinking water
应急出口	emergency exit
应急定位发射器	emergency locator transmitter
应急医疗箱	emergency medical kit
撤离滑梯	escape slide
撤离绳	escape strap
急救箱	First Aid Kit
目视信号装置	visual signal device
浮垫	floating cushion
漂浮刀	floating knife
救生索	flotation handle
剪刀	scissors
纱布绷带	gauze bandage
充气手泵	hand pump
救生环	heaving ring
充气阀门	inflate valve
救生筏说明书	life raft manual
定位灯	locator light
信号反射镜	mirror
氧气面罩	oxygen mask
碘酒	PV Iodine Swabs
修理包	repair kit
海水染色剂	sea dye marker
海锚	sea anchor
金属夹板	wire splint
口哨	whistle
水净化药片	water purification tablet
水驱动手电筒	water activated flashlight
救生手册	survival manual
三角巾	sterile triangular bandage
脱水海绵	sponge dehydrated
烟雾探测器	smoke detector

附录四　各国城市中英文简表

中　文	英　文	中　文	英　文
纽约	New York	伦敦	London
洛杉矶	Los Angeles	马德里	Madrid
圣弗朗西斯科	San Francisco	阿姆斯特丹	Amsterdam
夏威夷	Hawaii	布拉格	Prague
芝加哥	Chicago	莫斯科	Moscow
塞班岛	Saipan	布里斯班	Brisbane
多伦多	Toronto	凯恩斯	Keynes
温哥华	Vancouver	奥克兰	Auckland
悉尼	Sydney	成田	Narita
墨尔本	Melbourne	羽田	Haneda
仁川	Inchon	大阪	Osaka
曼谷	Bangkok	名古屋	Nagoya
新加坡	Singapore	福冈	Fukuoka
巴厘岛	Bali	札幌	Sapporo
马尼拉	Manila	静冈	Shizuoka
胡志明市	Ho Chi Minh City	冈山	Okayama
科伦坡	Colombo	新潟	Niigata
金边	Phnom Penh	那霸	Naha
吉隆坡	Kuala Lumpur	广岛	Hiroshima
巴黎	Paris	小松	Komatsu
法兰克福	Frankfurt	鹿儿岛	Kagoshima
罗马	Rome		

参考文献

[1] 赵恒. 客舱播音技巧 [M]. 北京：中国民航出版社，2016.
[2] 袁雯. 普通话水平测试指导用书 [M]. 2版. 上海：立信会计出版社，2011.
[3] 汪小玲，杨青云. 空乘服务沟通与播音 [M]. 北京：国防工业出版社，2017.
[4] 王丽蓉，胡妮. 机上广播英语 [M]. 北京：清华大学出版社，2018.
[5] 范晔，邹海鸥. 空中乘务情景英语 [M]. 北京：清华大学出版社，2018.
[6] 王桂珍. 英语语音教程 [M]. 2版. 北京：高等教育出版社，2005.
[7] 刘宇，倪贤祥. 英语语音教程 [M]. 成都：西南交通大学出版社，2016.
[8] 郭大伟. 英语的句子重音 [J]. 疯狂英语（教师版），2013（2）：169-220.
[9] 范建一. 民航乘务英语实用会话 [M]. 北京：中国民航出版社，2014.